Risk Less
Spend More

Everything
You
Never
Learned
About
Retirement

by

Tom Penland

Copyright © by Tom Penland

All rights reserved. No part of this book may be reproduced, copied, stored, shared, translated, distributed or transmitted in any printed or electronic form, or by any means whatsoever graphic, electronic, or mechanical, including but not limited to photocopying, scanning, recording, or information storage and retrieval system without the prior written permission of the Author.

Please see additional professional disclaimer on page 168.

First Edition, 2017,

1 2 3 4 5 6 7 8 9 10 LSI 22 21 20 19 18 17
Set in Cambria and Garamond.

Photographs on page xxii, xxiii, are owned by the Author.

Images and icons in this book are in the public domain.

International Standard Book Number: 978-0-9913381-7-7

TOM PENLAND, RICP®
Greenline Associates, CEO/Founder
www.greenlineca.com

Financial Blog
www.risklessspendmore.com

CONTENTS

Preface — vii
Introduction by Tom Penland

Chapter 1.	New Rules Apply	1
Chapter 2.	Retirement Planning Is 'Spending' Planning	20
Chapter 3.	Get Your Assets Together	32
Chapter 4.	Risk—Look Before You Leap	46
Chapter 5.	Hope, Human Nature and Retirement	64
Chapter 6.	Ready-Set-Go!	81
Chapter 7.	Safety First	92
Chapter 8.	Building Your Retirement Pyramid—Social Security	98
Chapter 9.	Build Your Foundation To Last	112
Chapter 10.	Knowing Vs. Hoping	143
Chapter 11.	Risking It All… On Red	154
Chapter 12.	Taking Charge	163

Epilogue — 167
Professional Disclaimer — 168

ACKNOWLEDGEMENTS

Firstly, I want to thank my dear mother and grandmother for the part of their lives they gave so that my brothers and I could have the lives we have. It was not an easy life and they sacrificed much. If not for their limitless love and care, I would not be who I am and this book would not have been written. I am grateful for the lessons I learned from them, the ability to think for myself and the common sense that I genetically inherited from them. I am grateful for the support and vote of confidence from my two sons, Canaan and Easton.

Thanks to all my workshop and class attendees for the time they have taken to attend the courses I teach, and for learning those, too infrequently taught lessons. I also want to acknowledge them for the intelligent, probing questions they have asked, to educate themselves and make good decisions. These questions have helped me to be a better educator and a better advisor.

Lastly, but certainly not least, thank you to Loren Blumberg, George Ivy, Alice Joyce, Joe Dismondi, Lowell Roberts, and Ron Castles. These are some of my loyal, unwavering and conservative minded clients that spent precious time helping me in the first edit of this book. They helped me to clarify my message and thereby, they have helped you too.

PREFACE

"To Boldly Go Where No Man Has Gone Before..." was the infinitive-splitting opening narration for each episode of Star Trek. Though you will not be going it alone, retirement that is, you will need to go boldly. It will not be the retirement of our parents. They were likely to work for the same company all, or almost all their working years. If they had a good job, they received a good pension upon retirement. If they had a great job, they likely received a great pension. Most of our parents were not investors—they were savers. When they retired, they had dependable and guaranteed Social Security income with a real cost-of-living increase. They had guaranteed lifetime income from their pension. And they had their savings for extras and emergencies. Usually they had their house paid off, held little (if any) debt, and focused on living a modest, comfortable, and relatively stress-free retirement life. That was then; that was them. We are different, and times today are significantly different.

Most people have not worked for the same company their entire career. Most people do not have a pension. Most 55-and-uppers have qualified plans, such as a 401(k), IRA, 403(b), TSP (as well as others), and we do not know whether those accounts will be worth more or less in the future. Not in the short term, even—let alone the long term. Our parents knew they were going to be okay in retirement, but most retirees' today hope they are going to be okay.

Most retirees live on the edge, their sense of financial security hijacked by market ups and downs. Though we still have the benefit of Social Security, we no longer have a real cost-of-living adjustment. Retirees must deal with that. We do not even know if we can count on Social Security 100%, and we cannot be sure of receiving 100% of our Social Security for the rest of our lives. Lacking the guarantees our parents had with Social Security and pensions, we must know what to do with our personal finances. Our retirement nest egg, our 401(k) and other like, tax-deferred accounts are everything when it comes to retirement success. It is the make-or-break for peace of mind and security. Retirement is a much different scenario in our day than in our parents' day. Sometimes it seems like a financial mine field—difficult to maneuver if you don't know where the mines are. In the series, Star Trek, one of Mr. Spock's often-stated responses was "highly illogical". I think that after reading this book you will find the appropriate answer to the question, 'was the 401k developed for us, for the purpose of protecting us, for the purpose of providing us a secure source of retirement income' will also be "highly illogical."

Most pre-retirees and retirees today are very concerned about having enough money to live on for the rest of their lives. Money means independence. It allows us to maintain our dignity. The money we have at retirement represents our time, our talents, and our discipline. How we manage that money will determine what we eat, where we live, what we drive, what we wear, where we go, what we leave to others, and a whole lot more. What we do with that money now will determine our lifestyle, security, and peace of mind—or lack thereof—for the rest of our lives.

But the truth is, it takes more than accumulated money to meet your minimal living requirements and provide for your lifestyle goals and desires. We think of our retirement years. We *dream* of our retirement plans unfolding just as we hoped. We consider our ability to pay increasing healthcare costs. We wonder whether the growth of our assets will continue. We worry whether we will have sufficient income to live on once we are no longer working. All these musings are founded on a single assumption; our retirement success must depend on market outcomes, election results, Fed actions, world events, and many other issues outside our control.

Though these matters *can* play a large part in your retirement success, the much bigger factor is YOU! How your life unfolds, what happens to your money—decisions *you* make about your savings impact your retirement success much more than all the factors outside your control.

How your life unfolds, what happens to your money—decisions you make about your savings impact your retirement success much more than all the factors outside your control. No, that wasn't a misprint. I meant to repeat that sentence. Why? Because this fact is too often overlooked. As you read the rest of this book you will learn why it is true. And that's good news—because it means you have a lot more control than you may think.

Decisions you make (or fail to make) will largely determine how much you get to spend, whether you pay more taxes than you need to, and how much you can leave to others. Ultimately, your decisions will determine whether you battle stress or enjoy peace of mind during your golden years. Sadly, most people spend more time planning their vacation than planning their retirement. They never figure out their current financial state—much less where they want to be and how to get there. Since you are reading this book, you are likely not one of those people! That is more good news for you.

Mistakes in your early working years can often be corrected. But the retirement years are different. Say you start off retirement having done everything right; you have accumulated retirement assets, maintained spending discipline in line with your working income, and obtained home equity. You are part of the fortunate few. Even so, *you only get one chance to do retirement right.* You cannot wake up at age 80, out of money, and start over. It doesn't work that way. The financial time horizon for retirement is short. We are no longer saving; we are spending what we saved. The terrain is different. Thus, retirement is a time to change financial gears. You must transition from earning years into spending years, preserving and allocating what you have earned so that it provides the most spendable dollars—and therefore the most life—for your money. Retirement is a time of making decisions that provide the maximum income, of making sure your assets last for the rest of your lifetime.

Let me emphasize one more time, your retirement success depends on you more than *anything* else. In fact, it depends on you more than everything else; the market, the global economy, elections, the Fed, interest rates, and the like. It depends on how you invest, how and where you allocate your nest egg, how much risk you take, how much certainty you build into your plan. It depends on how you spend your assets (and in what order). It depends on getting the right information so you can make the best Social Security claiming decision. These are the important decisions every 55-and-upper must consider so they can maximize spending, minimize taxes, and live the most life possible in retirement.

We are possibly looking toward many years of very low interest rates—or possibly even negative interest rates. Some countries already have employed negative interest markets in an effort to maintain some growth in their economy. The fact that Janet Yellen (Chair of the U.S. Federal Reserve) has even mentioned the words "negative interest rates" may not bode well for the U.S. economy. Unlike our parents, who earned good rates of interest on savings, we will slowly go broke if we hold most of our money in the bank today. The other side of the coin is that if we do not have low rates, we will likely have higher inflation. Add to that the ever-present market volatility working against you. All in all, *knowing what to do with your assets has never been more important.* We have never seen a time where the difference between making good decisions and bad decisions will have such a huge and dramatic impact on how people live in their retirement years.

It is not a matter of whether you need to put your money to work or not. You do! Rather, it is a matter of knowing enough to put those assets to work in a manner aligned with: (1) who you are; (2) the amount of assets you have; and (3) where you want to go, financially speaking. This book won't make decisions for you, but it will provide you with another side of retirement planning. It's another direction, another option, a more conservative approach than what you have been taught until now. I warn you, reading this book will change the way you think about your hard-earned money going forward. At a minimum, it will shake up the 50-year-old, "same old same old" stuff you have been told—and have been sold.

For a long and secure retirement, the biggest planning challenge is getting ready for the day you stop working. Combined with that is the need to turn your assets, at that point into an income stream *you cannot outlive.* This new financial challenge is different from any you have faced before. Frankly, it is the most important. Remember—no redo's. Plain and simple, if your required gross income is $7,000 per month and your Social Security is going to provide $4,000, you need to answer this question, "Where is the rest coming from?" Not just on Day One, but for the rest of your life. Oh, plus the increase you will need for inflation.

Social Security alone presents the retiree with untold complexities affecting when to file for benefits and what strategy to use. There are hundreds of strategies for how to structure all your assets (individual retirement accounts [IRAs, 401(K)s life insurance policies, annuities, investment portfolios). On top of that, everyone is different. Their situations, goals, desires, and objectives are different. Their envisioned retirement is unique to them. So, figuring out how to make the most of your money will require some work. Though you will obviously require some professional help, remember, no financial professional can do anything to help you without your help. This is a team effort; maybe the most important one of your life. Be willing to participate. You will need to devote time to gathering information, educating yourself or being educated, and thinking and talking through these important financial issues with your financial professional.

Your parents had a pension. You must figure out how to create your own "pension" with what you have. Though we know the day is coming when we will no longer work, and though most people are more than a little concerned about having enough money to live comfortably, not everyone is willing to exert effort to get the most from their retirement assets. Most people put it off, tending to less important matters. Life has many distractions. But retirement is your life (or soon will be). Efforts you expend now are the seeds you sow—for a harvest you are depending on for the rest of your life. Education and the help of a financial professional (one specifically trained in how to make the most of your money in the "spending years") will go a long way towards obtaining for you the retirement life you desire. To use my final Star Trek quote, the intent is for you to, "live long and prosper".

The retirement years are not for the faint of heart. Aging, and enjoying it, requires courage. In the end, I do not think many of us will be lying on our final bed wishing we had more money. We will be wishing we had more life. Life is way more valuable than money—

so live it. Live it today. Retire as soon as you can comfortably do so. As I say, "Bolder not older." You can do *almost anything you want* in retirement. Do it!

INTRODUCTION

"Tom, the police are taking Michael out in handcuffs." My co-worker's voice came through the phone loud and clear, 30 days after the stock market crash on October 19, 1987. I was a stockbroker, a registered representative for a large brokerage firm in Cleveland, Ohio. Michael was the top-producing broker in our office, situated right across the hallway from me.

"Beer here! Cold beer!" were the next words I heard Michael speak. It was almost two years later at a Cleveland Browns and Pittsburgh Steelers football game. His securities license had been revoked ... and he was selling beer. That's how it went in the "Good Ol' Days." Since then things have gotten better. Better for Wall Street that is. For Main Street, for the rest of us, for most hardworking people hoping to retire safely someday, not so much. Baby boomers nearing and in retirement have been dealt financial myths, half-truths, and a good amount of misdirection, all in the form of "conventional wisdom."

Have you ever wondered why pensions disappeared? Who benefitted from their disappearance? Hmmm. Think about it, who benefits when a bunch of inexperienced people are incentivized to get into the stock market game? After pensions went the way of the dinosaur, why was the only real option you had to save for retirement a 401(k) or some other tax-deferred account spelled R I S K? How did so many people end up with "investments" when they never really considered themselves investors? Owning investments makes you an investor no more than owning a hammer makes you a carpenter.

These are some of the questions that have occurred to me over the years since my stockbroker days in the early '80s. They are questions that have been highlighted and magnified by the hundreds of thousands of retirees and near-retirees who lost 50% or more of their retirement nest eggs in 2000-2002 and 2008. Something was clearly not right, to say the least. And it is still not right. Because, nothing has changed for the better. The hardworking 55-and-uppers who have saved for retirement are potentially at great risk. Very few can survive a loss of half their assets as they approach or experience retirement.

Returning to my years as a stockbroker, I was advising people to invest with me and invest with my company in the early '80s. Those were great years for the stock market. The financial tide was coming in and all boats were rising—including my clients' boats. I started to believe I knew something. I started to think I was good! My clients were happy because they were making money. My first son, Canaan, was born. Life was good.

But once the big crash hit in October 1987, my confidence was shaken. I received a barrage of phone calls from hardworking mom-and-pop business owners, widowed spouses, and retired auto workers. They kept asking me, "Tom, what are we going to do now? We have lost so much of our money." I started to realize something was amiss.

That was when I learned the meaning of the phrase, "A rising tide lifts all boats." The tide rose in the early '80s and my clients' financial boats rose with it. But then that tide quickly retreated, taking with it large portions of my clients' money. They were left high and dry, gasping for air like fish out of water.

I was not too concerned at first. Remember now, this was the first significant crash since I had become a stockbroker. Early on following the crash I recall telling worried and nervous people: "Don't worry. The analysts that get paid the really big money, the ones who advise us brokers on how to advise you clients, they will surely tell us what to do." Well, the top-down help never materialized, and I became very concerned. My colleagues said to me, "Hey, as stockbrokers, we get paid to sell stocks, bonds, and mutual funds. The market goes up and the market goes down. We make money either way." That's when I realized the system wasn't set up to make money for the investing client. It was set up to make money for the company and those 'selling' what the company wanted sold. Shocking, right?

As a matter of fact, my managing supervisor reminded me that I was employed by the company. *They* were signing my check, *not the client.* I was told that I worked for the company, and I was there to increase the profit of the company. My task was to sell more stocks, more bonds, and more mutual funds—come hell or high water, whether the market was going up or down. My job was first and foremost to make money for the *stockholders!* My supervisor did offer a very weak defense "Now, we do not intentionally want to hurt anyone ... but sometimes it happens." Wow! Being so callous about potentially ruining someone's life in the name of profit. Really? Hard to believe the self-deception and financial indoctrination was so subtle that these people somehow thought they were honorable.

I also came to realize that my firm (and all firms) had a list of "mega clients:" investors with millions instead of thousands. The mega clients were given different advice than what I was told to give to my clients. And my clients were the mom-and-pop business owners struggling 60+ hours a week to build a business; the auto workers on the assembly lines, the engineers, the school teachers, and the already-retired folks counting on me to see them through. I was dismayed and disappointed to realize that among my stockbroker peers, I was the only one very upset about my clients' losses. I no longer had confidence in what I was told to sell every day. So I found myself spending many hours researching and coming up with what I hoped would be good advice going forward.

How do you think that turned out? Sometimes my ideas were good, and sometimes they were not—exactly like everyone else. Did you know that the top money managers in any given year are not the top managers the year before or the year after? These people are all trying to convince you they can get you bigger returns than the next guy.

Eventually, my worries about losing other people's money—money they were going to need—started keeping me up at night. The handwriting was on the wall for me. Yes, my career as a stockbroker was left behind as we moved out of the '80s. Thomas Edison once said, "There is a better way for everything. Find it." Like that, I was determined to find a better way to save and to invest, both for myself and for those I advised.

Introduction

Before continuing, I want to be very clear. I do not see anything wrong with investing in stocks, bonds, and mutual funds. The huge potential for disaster comes from teaching, insinuating, and brainwashing hard working Americans so that they come to 'believe' the only way to make money is to have all of your savings at risk. Otherwise sane, mostly-conservative to moderately-conservative people have been harmed by the way market investments have been portrayed and sold.

Also, investments are often sold for the wrong reason, to the wrong person, at the wrong time. Why? So the broker, the advisor, or the agent can get paid. This is true not only for stocks, bonds, and mutual funds, but also for life insurance, annuities, and every other investment product.

There is a war going on, a battle for your retirement dollars. Wall Street, banks, insurance companies, advisors, and other financial professionals are all vying for your attention and ultimately your money. Making it worse, you have a multitude of what I will call financial 'un-professionals', which complicates the issue. It is ultimately important that you figure out who is truly in your corner. Find out what are you not being told, what could drastically affect your retirement lifestyle? What is it that you don't know that will determine whether you have enough to live on the rest of your life? What might result in a retirement of trying to figure out how to shrink your lifestyle to match your income, your diminishing spending power, year after year? What is your true risk tolerance? How much risk can your nest egg take before it is unable to be repaired? These are the questions you must demand answers for—honest answers.

The good thing is, as we get older we get wiser. We have perspective gained from a lifetime of reality. Some of he questions on every pre-retiree's mind are:
- Can I afford to retire?
- How much money can I afford to live on without running out?
- How much risk can I afford to take in retirement?
- Is there a way to have a dependable, secure strategy for income in retirement?

Introduction

- I have an employer pension. Should I take the lump sum or give up my money for the income? How do I make the best decision to create the most flexibility, and provide the most spendable dollars for the rest of my life?
- What are my options for a 401(k), IRA, or other qualified plans from my current or previous employer?
- What is the best way to take more control of 'other' retirement strategies by transferring 401(k), 403b, and other qualified employer-sponsored plan assets?
- What is the best time to start taking Social Security and the best claiming strategy?
- Should I protect some of my assets from loss? If so, how? And how much?
- How will I deal with the possibility of high-cost healthcare as I age?
- How much more income will I need because of inflation?
- How can I replace lost income when my spouse dies?
- Are there other income gaps in my future? What do I do about it?

This book is written to answer those questions for a particular type of person; the person who has learned at some point in life not to spend all the money they worked so hard for. This book is for those who have saved and invested; those who have exercised discipline, and who therefore have accumulated a retirement nest egg. Whether that nest egg is small or large, they want to take the right steps to develop and implement a strategy—one that will provide them the maximum spendable dollars in their retirement years, as well as minimize taxes whenever possible.

If that is your character, if you are asking the questions listed above, and if you are a 55-and-upper, then this book was unequivocally written for you. The intention is to help you answer these questions in a way such, that you *really* understand your options. I want you to hear "the rest of the story," as Paul Harvey used to say. Herein you will be provided new and valuable information that, unfortunately, most pre-retirees and retirees will never have the benefit of. This book will help you make decisions to secure much-needed and highly-desirable security, flexibility, options, and peace of mind. These decisions will be your decisions, based on a real understanding of risk and your true tolerance of risk (both psychologically and financially). They will be realistic decisions, based on the amount of money you have. They will be decisions based on knowing, not hoping.

Only a short generation ago the hope of retirees was, "I hope I live long enough to enjoy some retirement." Now that has become, "What if I live too long, and run out of money?" Today's 55-and-uppers are more worried about running out of *money* than they are about running out of *life*. Couple this with the reality that most retirees have saved for retirement inside a qualified plan: a 401(k), a 403b, a 457 plan, a thrift savings plan through their employer, or an IRA. This generation is preparing to retire with their money in stocks, bonds, and mutual funds—even though they do not consider themselves investors. They have little knowledge about such things. For that matter, they typically have little desire to gain knowledge about such things. Even when they do, they get more of the same, self-serving and biased info.

I know you have placed your faith, hope, trust, and retirement plans on the growth of the stock market. We have all been taught, and coerced into putting our 'blind faith' in the market. And that has created our predicament. We were given few or no other options for retirement savings. We were taught—make that *told*—to put our money into the market, because "it always goes up ... or at least goes back up." I'm certain you have heard the "You're in it for the long haul" conversation. That teaching was not entirely untrue, but I somehow doubt you ever heard it explained that the market "always goes down too ... or even back down." Or, how that affects what you actually earn for the risk you take.

FYI, when I use the term *the market* in this book, I am referring to the stock markets in general, including the Dow Jones, the S&P 500, the NASDAQ, and others. I am not referring to any particular market index. If I want to refer to a particular index, I will name it specifically.

Speaking of the market, many of you have experienced the elation of a booming bull market—as well as the terror and havoc of a fast-charging bear market. As a retirement income planning professional, I am often asked, "Do you think the market is going to go up or go down?" My reply is always the same, "Yes. Yes, the market is going to go up, and yes the market is going to go down." In truth, my job is not to predict and/or pretend that I know where the market is going. That was my job when I was a stock broker some years ago. My job was to convince people that I represented the best company and that I was the best person to grow their money. After the crash, I learned my job had really been to sell what I was told to sell and to pretend to be knowledgeable. That way, the firm I worked for could post higher profits, increase the value of their stock for the shareholders, and then brag about it.

Since leaving that position, I have learned there is a completely different way to grow your assets. There is a way to allocate your hard-earned assets so you have *true diversification.* There is a way for your hard-earned money to be *protected,* a way to grow some of your money by linking it to the market to provide gains (sometimes very good gains), and to not give it back when the market goes down! Protected investors who follow this way know the market sometimes generates cash like it's never going to stop. But they also know there are times it can demolish your wealth and your future. (Times like the scary bear markets of 2000-2002, 2008, and whatever year the next crash will be.)

The purpose of this book *is not* to convince you to invest zero money in the market. I have money invested in the market. The purpose of this book *is* to help you clearly understand that is it not a good idea to have *all* your money in the market (as Wall Street would like you to do). The biggest mistake a retiree can make is to spend money that has decreased in value. You are not only spending a dollar—you are spending two, three, four, or more dollars with each dollar you spend. (I'll give the full explanation later in the book.) The retirement years are the spending years. *Always have some money available that has not decreased in value* is one of the secrets protected investors have learned. And this knowledge can protect you too.

Despite all the financial books that have been written, despite the TV talking heads, despite the debacles of recent past, despite how much market realities have changed, despite all of that, most

55-and-uppers continue to hear the same old advice I handed out back in the '80s, as a stockbroker. You know, like "Buy and hold." Did you know that the average time held for many stock market purchases is less than 120 seconds? Huh? Why are we still being told, "Buy and hold"? There is a radical need for advice of a different sort. Advice that does not presume you will follow blindly. Rather, advice that respects the idea that financial peace of mind can only come from a degree of understanding. Financial peace of mind comes from understanding sufficiently to trust your own decisions.

I hope to present you an *insider's* view that will once and for all change your belief about the wisdom of risking all (or too much) of your hard-earned retirement money in the stock market. I also hope that because of a new, changed belief, your life in retirement will forever be altered—in a way I can feel good about having been a part of. Again, please know that my intention is not to scare you away from investing in the stock market. My intention is to teach you about *better ways to invest and diversify* than only stocks, bonds, and mutual funds. There is a far better way to allocate your assets for a successful retirement. This way provides *real* diversification rather than what I call "pixie dust diversification" (more on that later).

I thought about titling this book, *Retirement: When, How, Why, Who, Huh*. But the editor talked me out of it. That's okay, though I liked the title. I liked the title because I know that every 55-and-upper wants to know a few things.

- They want to know, WHEN can they retire?
- They want an answer for HOW they can retire—how their plan, a plan hopefully designed specifically for them by an expert, is going to work. How will it provide security and certainty?
- And they want to know WHY it works, because understanding provides peace of mind.
- To get there, they want to know WHO can help them. Who can they trust? Who really has the knowledge to best help them retire safely? Who has the compassion and patience to work through their questions and concerns?
- Last but not least, the HUH.
    - Huh, as in, what the hell just happened?

Introduction

    o Huh, as in the crashes of 2000–2002, 2008, and whatever crash comes next.

    o Huh, as in the drops of 50% many hopeful 55-and-uppers experienced, riding the market roller coaster up and down, with all their money in the seat next to them. YIKES!

    o Huh, as in the huge disconnect between what we have been taught and what really works.

    o Huh, as in the disconnect between Wall Street and the rest of us here on Main Street.

Even though I was talked out of my original title for the book, I will still provide the answers to these questions. You need the answers because a successful, less stressful future depends on it.

As a caveat, I do not intend to present a Henny-Penny, Chicken-Little, the-sky-is-falling alarmist view. But I must warn you in advance; presenting the alarming truth without causing alarm is difficult. I have only one small book, one small chance, to help you understand how to plan and secure your retirement years. We have only this brief time together.

And I must help you not only hear but also understand something very simple. Simple, yes—yet so counterintuitive it is hard to comprehend that... **You can make more money by risking less.** You can have more money to live on in retirement by risking less.

To stand a fighting chance of helping you truly understand, I cannot circle around the edges of the issues. I cannot beat around the bush. I must be clear and to the point. So, sometimes I will seem dramatic in my explanation. Drama is typically associated with fiction, but sometimes the truth is stranger than fiction. Plus, much of what you have learned is indeed fiction—especially when it comes to what is delivered up as *conventional wisdom.*

In this one little book, I am going to attempt to balance the 30-plus years of slanted and biased information most people have been blindly following. For me, it is an exhilarating and even provocatively big goal for a little book. That said, I am confident that together—you as the reader and me as the teacher—we will succeed. In our brief time together, I am confident I can open the window wide enough for long enough that you will more clearly view your retirement on the horizon. And I am also confident it will be a brighter, more joyful, more secure view than you had before this book!

Who am I to write this book? I am someone that has learned a great deal about the reality of money, growing money and converting it into income over the last 30 years. Though your financial faith may be challenged in this book, I am not some financial messiah, having come out of the wilderness to save you with a new financial religion. I am not some TV talking head trying to convince you to follow me and do what I say. I am someone who wants you to know *the rest of the story* so you can make the best retirement decisions for yourself, so you can save yourself. Save yourself from what? From the stress of worrying, for the next 25+ years, about running out of money. From lying awake at night, wondering how to further shrink your lifestyle to make ends meet from year to year. See, money allows us to maintain our independence and dignity in our retirement years. Ultimately, that is what we are worrying about when we say, "I am worried about running out of money." Lack of money equates to a lack of independence and dignity. It's the inability to take care of ourselves financially.

Left to Right: Pete, Tom (me), Jeff holding Brian, and Brett

Introduction

My Mother and I.

I am the second oldest of five energetic boys (second from the left). Maybe I should say, "Was." We are not as energetic as we used to be! We were raised mainly by a one-in-a-million single mom. She loved us so much it killed her. She died before her time, God bless her. And I do think her early demise had much to do with the fact that she worried too much about her boys and thought little about anything for herself. I dedicate this book to her. I love you, Mom. Thank you for all you did and for all you gave. My mom's mom, our grandmother, was a wonderful influence in our lives too. I believe that if at least one person in a child's life loves them unconditionally, they stand a good chance of succeeding in life. Well, we had two. If any good comes to you from this book, be grateful to my mother, Bonnie and Grandma Janie.

I grew up in a poor neighborhood in Cleveland, Ohio. We lived on the proverbial, wrong side of the tracks. I learned at a young age not to ask my mom for things she couldn't provide. It hurt me to see the sadness and disappointment in her eyes. I learned that if I wanted something, I would have to work for it. So, in elementary school

I drew horse heads and sold them for a nickel. Later I shoveled snow, mowed grass, and washed cars until I was 15. Then I got a job working 32 hours a week in the kitchen of the local hospital. There I learned how to value work, pitch in, take responsibility for myself, and help out. These invaluable lessons built my character. They had much to do with who I am today. No different than most of you, whom also learned similar character-building lessons in your own lives. They are lessons I have worked to impart to my two sons.

I am a person (probably like some of you) who overcame the neighborhood excuse to stay poor. "The rich are holding us down." You still hear it today—even louder, I think. I am not blind. I know the gap between the rich and poor is getting bigger. The gap between rich and middle class is growing too. Nevertheless, that psychological disempowerment via excuses is holding more people back than the rich ever could. I learned that I could do whatever I wanted to do if I worked hard enough to better myself. This was a much better life lesson than "the rich are holding you down." (Okay, I'm getting off my soapbox.)

I was also taught to help others when I could. And what I am doing right now is writing this book with the intention of changing some people's lives for the better. That could be a big 'help', especially in retirement. You only get one chance to do retirement right. I have been helping people save money, earn money, invest money, and manage money in one way or another since the early 1980s.

I am one of a pretty small number of Retirement Income Certified Professional (RICP®) designees. Typically, I am not too big on designations. The education to get them, yes! But I have seen designations used as a sales tool too often—as though you should trust someone because of their designations. But over the years, I have spent a not-so-small amount of money and time becoming educated in the field of personal finance. The only designation I value enough to continue to pay for and use is the RICP® designation. It is the newest, cutting-edge, premier education geared specifically for planning income in the retirement years—how to get the most out of what you have saved.

Some consider this designation the most respected certification in the income-planning arena. The excellent education it gave me has helped me to fine-tune the strategies I teach 55-and-uppers. It has helped me bring together a lifetime's worth of knowledge and real-world experience with the latest and greatest technology, tools, strategies, and retirement vehicles for saving and investing. Becoming an RICP® provided me with brand new and better ways to look at real risk tolerance, retirement asset allocation, and diversification. This new knowledge is one of the reasons I am writing this book, so I can share it with you. I hope you will make the absolute most of your nest egg; the money you have worked hard for, the money you have been disciplined enough to save.

So... who am I? I am the guy who learned at a young age to treat others the way I want to be treated. When it comes to my money, I don't want someone to tell me what to do with it. I want someone to help me know what to do with it. I don't want to tell you what to do with your money, I want you to know what to do with your money ... and make your own decisions. Does it not feel better to know what to do than to be told? Is it not better to know than to follow blindly, cross your fingers, and hope for the best?

I am the guy who became a single dad when my boys were 3 and 6, a guy who is proud they are now responsible and caring men who treat others the way they want to be treated. That's an accomplishment I had a significant part in—my life's most important accomplishment. Through them my life will continue to have an effect after I am gone. I am a guy who loves and knows the value of family.

I am a guy who has lived life and has had life 'happen' to him, like so many others. I am a guy that still believes in America, the one in "America the Beautiful." I am someone that is hopeful about the future. I am, I'll bet, a guy, a person very much like you. We want to do the right thing; we want to do our part. It's mostly what we've done up 'til now and it's what we are most likely to do for the rest of our lives. As I move into the last third of my life I want to be secure, I want to be comfortable. I don't want to worry about money. I don't want you to worry about money. We want to maintain our financial independence even when we may not be able to maintain our physical independence, right? Financial independence helps to preserve our dignity.

I am a guy who worked in a steel mill in the flats of Cleveland, Ohio. A guy who worked in the piston hook-up area of the 302-engine assembly line at Ford Motor Company. A guy who went to college, worked as a carpenter, waited tables, tended bar at the Grand Canyon, and hiked in the Grand Canyon many times—all before I was 28. I am a guy who wants to hike the Appalachian Trail someday. I was a real estate broker. I became a stockbroker more than 34 years ago. I am now an ex-stockbroker guy who realized that "selling" people on the idea that I knew better than anyone else how they could "beat the market," was not my thing. Furthermore, I am a guy who realized that this is a con. (I told you I don't have time to beat around the bush to make my point.)

Finally, who am I to write this book? I am a guy who learned a good bit from what didn't work like I was told it would. I learned from observing results versus all the hype. I am a guy who chose to believe nothing and verify everything—to go a different route. I am a guy who chose to find a better, safer way to plan for retirement ... my own retirement, and yours. That is "who I am" to write this book.

Tom Penland,
California, 2017

Chapter 1

New Rules Apply

New rules apply, and you would do well to learn them. This is not your father's retirement. The goals of more and more Americans have changed, particularly for 55-and-uppers. The new goals are:
- Protect my principal,
- Provide the income I need to live, and
- Protect me from the ravages of inflation.

As Americans enter or approach their post-career years, their focus shifts from earning wages and growing their assets to... preserving their hard earned nest eggs. They need to receive a steady stream of income from their nest eggs if they want to enjoy their lifestyle, while keeping their expenses in line with their income. They want to ensure their assets will provide enough to meet their lifetime needs and their lifestyle goals. Steady, secure income means financial independence and the maintenance of their dignity. Interest in developing a stable and dependable stream of cash has exploded in the last 10 years among pre-retirees, particularly as baby boomers have begun retiring.

Establishing and maintaining financial security and independence in those post-career years is not as easy job. Not that long ago, it was somewhat easier. Those were the days of *pensions,* the days when our *Social Security system* was secure. Back then it was fairly easy (financially speaking) to transition from the working years to the non-working, spending years.

Things are different now. Much has changed and continues to change in the economy, markets, government policies, and employer practices. The Federal Reserve has kept interest rates unrealistically low since 2008, they are printing money as fast as they can, and it will likely be years before rates return to any level that could provide retirement income and safety as it used to. Every chance they get, the government is cutting programs, minimizing cost of living increases for Social Security, means testing benefits we have paid for, and increasing fees and taxes—in ways most people are not even aware of. Wall Street and the markets aren't helping either. The old rules are gone and choices are becoming more complex.

All the factors surrounding a safe and secure retirement have changed or are changing. Tough and complicated decisions need to be made about IRAs, 401(k)s, medical insurance, investments, principle protection, asset allocation, risk, taxes, estate planning, and more. Some of these decisions are irreversible. Make a bad decision or two, and what's left of your retirement plan might not get you through the rest of your life. According to the Center for Retirement Research, "In 1989, only 30% of Americans ages 30 and older were on track to be financially prepared for retirement." In 2015, Things have not improved, with 52% of Americans over 30 were considered unlikely to be able to maintain their living standards in retirement and a large percentage of the remaining 48% are more than a little concerned about being prepared.

According to the Conference Board: About two-thirds of those aged 45–60 said in 2015 they will retire later than they had planned. In 2011, that number was only 42%.

Government data shows that after many years of declining, the average retirement age has been steadily on the rise. Many of those who think they're prepared for retirement are not.

Nearly half of all Americans die with financial assets of less than $10,000, according to recent research by MIT economist James Poterba. Many Americans enter retirement with seemingly substantial financial assets, but due to mistakes and unforeseen events they spend faster than they anticipated. And they never realize what is happening until it's too late.

This doesn't have to be your story. You can be financially secure during your post-career years, free of the worries that will plague so many. But you can't rely on what worked in the past, nor can you rely on what you are being told *might* work in the future. Following tired rules of thumb and traditional cookie-cutter approaches is not the road to income security. Rather, it is a road full of potholes and unanticipated hazards that will leave you wishing there was a 1-800-Retirement rescue line. Don't travel that road. Dozens of financial aspects for your post-career life have been or are being transformed, including the markets and economy, tax law, privacy, estate planning, health insurance, Medicare, Social Security, long-term care, annuities, and more. Your retirement strategies must be different from your working-years strategies. Moreover, you must use strategies and tools that are different from those that worked for *previous generations* of retirees, even those retiring only 10 years ago.

Baby boomers have been a unique part of the American story—blazing a trail, creating change, living with change thrust upon them. Baby boomers' retirement is no different. We must be the brave, we must embrace the change, and we must figure out how to make it work for us … lest it ultimately work against us. I mentioned previously that spending money that has diminished in value is a big no-no in the post-career years. Why? Because it is a threat to your lifetime income security. Threats to lifetime income security are the most perilous and must be addressed as early as possible. You must know how to deal with today's *six hazards on the road to lifetime income security*. Most of these threats are not new, but have been increasing—as has the danger to your financial security and future peace of mind.

Baby boomers (of which I am one) can take this journey together. We can blaze, yet another trail, showing our children and our generational peers that we are no shrinking flowers. We can show them how to live bravely and make wise decisions… how to be bolder… not just older.

THE SIX HAZARDS ON THE ROAD TO LIFETIME INCOME SECURITY

 Retirement Income Road Hazard #1- Not Our Parents' Social Security and Medicare.

Social Security and Medicare are bedrock institutions that have provided the secure financial foundation of retirement for decades. They will continue to be part of our foundation too. However, the programs are in financial trouble; they are changing and they will have to change even more. This foundation has been deteriorating for decades and is crumbling just as we prepare to build upon it for our retirement years.

You are not hearing about Social Security's problems for the first time. The problems are myriad, but there is no space to discuss them in depth here. Absent changes, the Social Security trust fund could be broke as early as 2030. A 25% cut in benefits (or more) will be required to maintain the system. The specifics of Social Security's financial condition and potential benefit cuts change annually as estimates are updated, but the general condition is not substantially changing in a way that would eliminate our worry. Many people say they don't expect to receive *anything* from Social Security and aren't including it in their retirement plans. That is a mistake, but a mistake that will not leave one in peril in later years. The *big mistake* is failing to plan for a reduction in Social Security. That will cause hardship and negatively impact life for many, at a time when they can do little about it.

Many people underestimate the importance of Social Security. Even for many higher-income people who earned the maximum Social Security wage base for 35 years, the program will provide only 28% of the pre- retirement income. For low-income beneficiaries, it replaces 90% of pre-retirement income. On average across our country, Social Security benefits are estimated to provide about 40% of the average retiree's income. Also, for many retirees Social Security has been the only income *indexed for inflation*. Baby boomers can no longer count on this benefit, as the federal government manipulates the CPI index to keep adjustments low or at zero. Most current retirees report depending more and more on Social Security as the years pass. When increases in their Social Security are few and far between, they tend to spend down other assets faster to make up the shortfall, and also to see the purchasing power of that other income dwindle because of inflation. Thus, you need to understand the role of Social Security and find the right financial professional to help you maximize your Social Security benefits.

If benefits are reduced—whether minimally or substantially— retirees will have to adjust. You may have heard that benefit reductions would likely be limited to those who are not already retired or are within 10 years of retirement, except for higher-income people. Two issues here:

1. That word "likely." Retirement security needs certainty and "likely" is not in that category.
2. "Except for higher income people." If you haven't noticed, every time politicians talk about the "wealthy" it ends up including those in the middle class—the people who have worked hard, maintained discipline, and saved for retirement. In other words, you. Sure, politicians talk about the one-percenters to rile everyone up. But then they make new laws and the law catches the middle class in its reach, and the one-percenters feel nothing.

My advice is to not give up on Social Security. Instead, realize its importance to your retirement. Plan to maximize and protect your benefits, but plan for a reduction. What if the reduction does not come? Then that will only improve your financial outlook; it will be icing on your retirement cake.

Medicare is in no better shape than Social Security. Without change, Medicare will be bankrupt as early as 2022, according to the Congressional Budget Office. As is always the case with government estimates and communications, the specific estimates change annually. Medicare is another important issue you will need to learn more about, but that is a different book.

A few changes have been made to the Social Security program in recent years, but more are certain. There are likely to be higher premiums, reduced benefits, more means-testing, and a later eligibility age. Social Security and Medicare have been the foundations of the American retirement, and we will have a tough time replacing them. Baby boomers are the beginning of the end for Social Security. Our parents got more security from this 'social' system than we will, and we will get more from it than our children will. They may get nothing. (They should be saving for that likelihood now.) In this book, you will learn what you can do for yourself to shore up your foundational Social Security income and plan to augment these benefits, as it will very likely become necessary. You'll learn to maximize the Social Security benefits you receive and avoid making the mistakes thousands of retirees make every year. Making the *right* and *best* decision about Social Security can potentially add tens of thousands of dollars to your nest egg.

Retirement Income Road Hazard #2- CAUTION! Most Retirement Investment Advice Is Wrong and Dangerous

Retirees and those close to retirement traditionally receive poor investment advice. Though demands from the Baby Boomers have forced some improvements in recent years, many still receive poor investment advice in the years immediately before and during retirement. That's not surprising. Most financial advisors and brokers concentrate on 'growth' for investors, not income which is what post retirement planning is about. Take note: These growth strategies do not work for clients once they enter the spending phase. Therefore, a new direction is needed. Spending is the opposite of accumulating. Retirees need to plan for the best way to provide income from their investments and hard-earned savings. They need to understand how to most effectively draw down (spend) their accounts so the accounts last as long as the retiree lasts.

Investment advice for retirees used to be simple, "As you age, move most of your portfolio into safe, income-producing investments such as short-term bonds, certificates of deposit, and money market funds. Then live off the income." That made sense when retirement lasted about five years, interest rates were higher, and you didn't have to worry about big changes in the cost of living. That was then. This is now and that same advice is dangerous to your retirement. More recently, retirees and pre-retirees were told to invest like everyone else, with "diversified" portfolios developed using historic returns, 'Monte Carlo' simulations, computer programs, and Modern Portfolio Theory. The dictionary defines *theory* as "a proposed explanation whose status is still conjectural and subject to experimentation, in contrast to well-established propositions that are regarded as reporting matters of actual fact." Is it only me, or does the word "theory" concern you when it is used in the same paragraph as retirement—*your* retirement? It should make you say, "Hmmmm."

Ever since the inception of 401(k)s we have been told to buy-and-hold these 'modern' portfolios (based on theory) and to count on the long-term trend of ever-rising stock prices to fund our retirements. That's a shame, and I will go, as far as to say it's a *sham*. (I told you I need to be dramatic to balance out what you have been told and have come to believe as fact.) The media's talking heads are constantly reminding us that the stock market has recently had an unparalleled period of growth. But what they never mention is that for our willingness to risk our money for the last 16 years, for our willingness to ride that roller coaster, close our eyes and grit our teeth and hold on for dear life, the results since 2000 have not been good. How can I say that? Well, aside from the additional money people have put into their 401(k), the average 55-and-upper has barely kept up with inflation. In other words, there has been no real gain in spending power. Not even after all this "unparalleled" growth. Is there any doubt why this strategy is in serious doubt and being questioned by many astute 55-and-uppers? It needs to be reconsidered.

In the day-to-day lives of retirees, this strategy often produces poor results. It leaves post-career individuals and families living on money that has decreased in value, thereby putting them in jeopardy of losing their retirement security. People in or near retirement should not invest as if they are still earning an income. The next 10 years matter most to them, not historic averages of the last 80. Investment returns in the five years immediately before and after retirement typically impacts your retirement the most. Realize that these shorter-term horizons make the old and stale advice of yesterday riskier than most baby boomers realize.

Here's another problem with most investment advice. People are told they have diversified portfolios when they really don't. The truth is that when a portfolio is 60% stocks or stock funds and 40% bonds or bond funds, 100% of their money is tied to what happens in the financial world, the political world as well as many other variables. Thus, all their money is subject to unknown volatility. Your retirement security rises and falls with these variables. When the bulls are running it can be exciting to see the account grow, but the drawdowns and losses since 2000 have hurt many retirees. Moreover, they have put future retirees in uncomfortable situations, unsure what to do or where to turn. Since 2000 we have had two of the biggest bull market run-ups in the market's history. I repeat to make a point; after inflation and fees, the money in most portfolios won't even buy as much as it did in 2000, excluding the additional money you have added or saved.

Anyone thinking they can live on a portfolio of volatile assets with confidence may have a very unpleasant awakening—and, at a time when it will be too late to do anything about it. You must not put yourself into a position where you have to spend money from your portfolio that has gone down in value due to market risk. That is a big retirement no-no!

These days, investing conservatively isn't rewarding either, thanks to the Federal Reserve board's low-interest-rate policy and market manipulation. The Fed is "saving the economy" by punishing hardworking savers and those who simply want a comfortable and secure retirement income. Savers are losing money after inflation and taxes. Fortunately, there are some relatively new options to take the place of the traditional safe and low-interest investments that use to work for our parents. These newer options can provide more security for the long term while eliminating much of the risk associated with the short term. You don't have to bounce up and down with the stock indices or sit on cash, losing money to inflation and taxes from your nest-egg assets. (This will be covered in a later chapter.)

 Retirement Income Road Hazard #3- Will the Real Inflation Rate Please Stand Up?

"The problem is, Tom, we didn't realize how much everything would cost. That is a big, big mistake we made." Those were the words of a 77-year-old man. He and his wife retired early, at 64 and 62, with the confidence that they would enjoy a long retirement. They had two modest pensions, Social Security, a home paid off in Manhattan Beach, CA, and a nest egg over $2 million. A mere 13 years later they were sitting across the desk from me, both healthy and active—with under $350,000 remaining. How would they be able to maintain their lifestyle? They weren't desperate for money, yet. But the couple was concerned that they had seriously underestimated the cost of retirement. And they had. They might live another 15 or more years, which are likely to be the most expensive years. He was hoping to find some part-time consulting work, though his wife was not keen on the idea.

This situation is not unusual. Ask retirees in their late 70s and early 80s, "What was your biggest retirement planning mistake?" A high percentage will say, "We estimated retirement spending poorly and failed to ensure that we had enough income—not only to last, but also to keep pace with inflation." As a financial professional, I see this all too frequently.

Retirement services company TIAA-CREF (Teachers Insurance and Annuity Association—College Retirement Equities Fund) surveyed adults who have not yet retired. They asked, "What percentage of your pre-retirement income do you expect to need in retirement?" One-third of respondents said they expect to need 25–50% of their pre-retirement income, while another third estimated 50–75%. Here's the traditional rule of thumb used by financial advisors; your annual retirement spending will be about *80% of your pre-retirement income.* That is well above the estimate many people use—but it actually, is not a good way to estimate your retirement spending either.

My financial practice is in Torrance, California. I almost *never*—and I mean never—have pre-retirees in the Southbay area tell me they expect to need less than their working income to live on in retirement. Life is expensive everywhere, but Southern California can be an extra burden on expenses. I think the 80% rule of thumb is one of the great myths of retirement planning, and it gets many people into trouble. Sure, you will spend less in retirement on expenses such as commuting, new work clothes, payroll taxes, 401(k) contributions, and a few other items. But since you aren't working, you have time to fill, and more life to live. That time might be filled by activities that cost money: golf, travel, entertaining, eating out, shopping, attending shows and movies, hobbies, spoiling the grandchildren, and a host of other possibilities. You are also likely to incur higher medical expenses over time. With parents living longer and children requiring more financial support, you may end up needing to assist both your parents and your children.

In my professional experience, most people's expenses stay the same or increase in the first years of retirement. If you plan to spend less (because of a rule of thumb that does not apply to your life) but end up spending more, this is a very big "oops" that can harm you right out of the gate.

Here's one good rule of thumb. The higher your income relative to the average, the less likely your expenses are going to decline in the first years of retirement. If you don't want to wake up in a cold sweat worrying about money only a few years into retirement, ignore the general rules. The question is; how much are *you* likely to spend in retirement? Many people learn that the general rules of thumb don't apply to them. We will talk further about how to estimate retirement spending in a later chapter.

Even many pre-retirees who correctly estimate their retirement spending fail to consider how inflation affects the purchasing power of income and assets over time. This is a huge oversight and can imperil an otherwise good income plan. In fact, failing to consider the effects of inflation is one of the most common retirement planning mistakes. Many people develop a spending plan for the first year or two of retirement that matches their income. But they forget that *costs change over time.* Inflation is one of the great road hazards on the retirement income road. The average 3% annual inflation of the last few decades *cuts your purchasing power in half* over 24 years, and by close to 20% after a mere 5 years. A more modest 2% inflation cuts your standard of living by 20% after 10 years. This loss does not happen overnight, but over time it becomes painfully obvious.

By the way, don't use the Consumer Price Index to measure inflation. It measures inflation for a basket of goods purchased by a hypothetical American family—*very* hypothetical. Apparently, the hypothetical family does not eat or spend money on utilities or gasoline for their car(s), since these things are not taken into account when calculating the CPI. Everyone's household spending is different, and so is their 'personal' inflation rate. For example, if your home is paid off, you will spend less on housing than you will on medical care. If you rent, you are likely to pay a lot for both, as prices continue to rise. There are many other spending differences from household to household. For some retirees, building in a 1% inflation factor for the future may be sufficient. For others, 3% may not be enough. Everyone has their own personal inflation rate. You will learn the right way to estimate your retirement expenses later in this book.

In the early 80s we used a 4–5% annual rate of inflation. From 1962 through 1982 the average was 5.9%. From 1982 until 2002 the rate was only (only, ha!) 3.2%. The table below indicates how much more money you will need based on differing rates of inflation. For example, at 4% inflation you will need 2.2 times more income in 20 years, assuming expenses remain constant. So, if your income need is $6,000 per month when you retire it would be $13,200 in 20 years. Calculating the annual numbers based on the CPI index and the annual reporting of inflation numbers *used to be sacrosanct and accurate.* They were something you could count on for projecting future needs. Now the annual reported inflation is no longer trustworthy; the numbers are manipulated to reflect a rosier than 'real' picture. This is dishonesty perpetrated upon the citizens by their government, as if saying something made it true. Shocking, right? Beware, you have been warned.

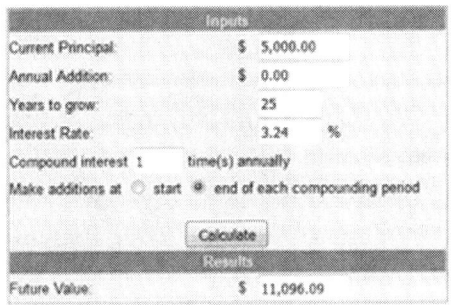

Since 1924 the average inflation has been 3.24%. The possibility, maybe even the reality is that; if you need $5,000 per month to live on today, and based on that, in 25 years you would need $11,096.

 Retirement Income Road Hazard #4- What If I Live Too Long?

Not all that long ago, we worried about not living long enough as we approached retirement. Now many people worry about just the opposite; living beyond their money. For the first generation of post-World-War-II retirees, retirement generally lasted five years or so. Today, many people still mistakenly believe they must plan for fewer years than the reality. Twenty-year retirements are common, and thirty-year retirements are not unusual. People on average still retire around age 65. Although many people now say they plan to work longer, and the average retirement age has been increasing, about half of people retire involuntarily and before they expected to. It is no secret that people are living longer than they used to. Here's a sample of what you need to know about longevity. Considering a married couple who both turned 65 today, there is a 20% chance one spouse will live to age 95. If both are still alive at 80, the odds will increase by about 50% (according to the insurance actuaries). Many people born in 1946 and later can expect to spend more than 30 years in retirement. Some will spend more time in retirement than they did in their careers.

Here's another twist to consider: Life expectancy increases with wealth and education. The wealthier and better educated a person is, the greater on average is their life expectancy. Such a person may have access to better medical care and is more likely to make smarter lifestyle choices. The person's career probably was not as physically demanding and was unlikely to result in injuries or disability. These factors increase the potential of an above-average lifespan—probably about four years longer than the average for his or her age. Lifespans are likely to increase in coming years as science discovers new treatments and cures.

There are many benefits to longevity and longer lifespans, but there is also one giant negative. *The nest egg needed to pay for all those years of retirement can be substantial.* It is paramount to your financial security that you not only protect your nest egg from loss but also grow it at the pace of inflation. Only by so doing will you be able to pay for years of retirement and protect your purchasing power from decades of inflation.

 ## Retirement Income Security Threat #5- You're On Your Own For Medical Care

There was a time when we used to look forward to Medicare kicking in for our healthcare at age 65. Patients were respected and the care was excellent and plentiful. Again, those days are over. We are in real turmoil with healthcare. As of this writing, the Affordable Care Act is in uncertain condition. Even if it stands for the long haul, the coverage is more expensive and covers less—much less in some cases. Medicare reimburses many doctors very little so they avoid Medicare patients. Except in rare circumstances, the respect shown by spending quality time with a patient is gone. The doctors no longer have the time. They must see more and more patients to earn a living now.

Most Americans worry about retirement medical and long-term care costs. Near 67% of Americans ages 55 to 65 said medical expenses were the top retirement concern (according to a 2012 survey by Allianz). Many other surveys over the years reported similar results, and rightly so. Medical expenses are one of the retirement plan wild cards. This top concern is directly connected to the question, "Will I have enough income?"

Medical expenses and health care are among the most misunderstood and underestimated expense for retirees. Consider this; many Americans believe that Medicare or their employer's insurance will cover most retirement medical expenses and long-term care expenses they need. That's not even close to the truth. Only 28% of employers with more than 200 employees provide retiree medical coverage (compared to 66% in 1968). Most of those that still offer retirement medical benefits are reducing benefits and moving retirees to privately-run insurance exchanges. Smaller employers often provide no retirement medical benefits.

Currently, Medicare pays only 80 percent of covered expenses. You are on the hook for 20 percent of covered expenses with no limit, and we do not know what the future will bring. Plus, Medicare does not cover many medical expenses. You need to figure out ways to pay for all those types of medical costs. Medicare covers only about half of the average member's annual medical expenses. The typical retiree will pay $6,000–$8,000 out-of-pocket each year for medical care (estimates vary). Some will pay more and some will pay considerably more. On average, a married couple who both turn 65 today will need more than $270,000 over the next 20 years to pay for their medical expenses not covered by Medicare. Of course, those who have above-average needs or live past age 85 will need even more funds. Medicare generally does not cover long-term care expenses.

The truth is, Medicare pays for only 25% of total nursing home expenses in the United States. And those payments are largely for short-term rehabilitation after an illness or injury. Residents, their families, and Medicaid pay most nursing home expenses. Most prescription drugs are not covered by basic Medicare Parts A and B.

Medicare has begun means-testing too. The higher your income is, the higher your Medicare premiums will be for both traditional Medicare Part B and for prescription drug coverage under Part D. The Affordable Care Act shifts money away from Medicare, especially the popular Medicare Advantage program, reducing benefits and increasing costs for beneficiaries. Medical expenses will be one of the three biggest post-career expenses for most people, and they will only increase as the years go on. Even many of those who understand they are largely on their own for medical care need to know more than they do. Many pay too much for Medicare supplement, Part D prescription drugs, and long-term care insurance. Recent surveys found that many owners of these policies pay *up to twice what they need to.* You need to stay up to date regarding developments in Medicare, Part D prescription drug coverage, long-term care, and every other aspect of paying for retirement medical care. You need a knowledgeable Medicare advisor; someone you can count on and review with each year.

Retirement Income Road Hazard #6- Your Taxes Won't Go Down in Retirement

It used to be a truism that "taxes and tax rates will decline in retirement," as income tended to be less after retirement. Plus, Social Security income was not always taxable. That's no longer the case. Today, taxes and tax rates are less likely to decline after retiring. In many cases, a person's marginal income tax rate increases in retirement, and retirees face some of the highest marginal tax rates of their lives. Average tax rates are likely to stay the same or increase. You must be on constant guard against politicians devising new, creative and deceptive ways to get their hands on your nest egg. It's only going to get worse as the population ages. The bottom line is that for most retirees, taxes are one of the three largest items in their budgets. Most everyone, including the experts, feel the situation is likely to get worse. Congress and state and local governments are far more likely to increase your taxes than to cut them. Even if taxes do not increase, Uncle Sam will get more money from us one way or another. As an example, the Affordable Care Act was challenged all the way to the Supreme Court as a tax. It doesn't matter what you call it, though—it costs hardworking people more money. It takes money from working people and from employers, then gives it to the government in order to pay for others' health coverage. By any usual definition, when you take money (e.g. charge via healthcare law) from one person to pay for a benefit for another person, *that is a tax!* This makes effective tax reduction strategies important in retirement.

Conclusion

Yes, there are hazards on the retirement road that can and will negatively impact your income if you are not properly prepared. These hazards will affect your lifestyle, your peace of mind, and virtually almost everything else in your retirement life. Here's the good news; you can create safe, secure, sustainable, and dependable lifetime income. You don't have to sit helplessly by and let these roadblocks destroy your nest egg. You can get educated, be courageous, and make prudent decisions in anticipation of the hazards ahead. You can build a wall of protection around your nest egg assets to generate a reliable cash flow for when you need it.

As of this writing, the stock market indices are up. Most people have regained what they lost in 2008, and [maybe] gained a little bit more. By taking advantage of recent changes and income strategies, I believe today is a great opportunity for those who recognize the realities and prepare for retirement. Everyone's circumstances are different; their situation, assets, goals, and objectives are all different. No silver bullet or single ideal investment or one right strategy will work for everyone. But you can attain retirement success! I see it every day in my practice. You must take time to look past the gimmicks, fads, and stale old ideas that do not work in today's world. You must bypass the mass misdirection. But again, you can do it! You can create a successful retirement by using a financial toolbox of dependable strategies and a solid plan. And yes, there is an investment tool out there that will provide you the peace and security you desire for your golden years. Later chapters of this book will identify and explain them further.

Ignore the status quo, conventional rules of thumb, and the typical, standard Wall Street advice. The simpler and more certain the strategy, the better. You need to push past the complexity so beloved by Wall Street and Washington to find strategies that will maximize your cash flow and minimize your taxes.

Remember, a retirement plan is just that, a *plan*. A roadmap, if you will. The goal is to map out your financial future; act now to prepare for the trip, remain flexible, and adjust as life unfolds. Retirement planning is not set-it-and-forget-it. Just like AAA can prepare a TripTik to help you map out the best route across the country, identify sightseeing destinations, and plan exciting experiences, the right financial professional can do the same for your retirement road map. Someone who focuses on retirement issues will be the best prepared to keep you aware of changes, carefully analyze how those changes affect you, and recommend a course of action that will work for your specific goals and needs.

We know that retirement in the future will be as different from the retirement of the past as night is from day. Those who planned for retirement only 15 or 20 years ago, would be shocked by the task faced by their counterparts today. Many of the issues and questions, to be addressed today weren't even on the radar screen not all that long ago.

The first real generation of American retirees, those who retired in the 1960s and 1970s, developed the image of retirement that many Americans still hold today. You must get past that. For the second, third, and fourth retirement generations, things will be different. Sometimes they will be shockingly different. Many observers paint a gloomy picture of retirement in the coming years. Yet there is no reason for most people to experience a retirement that is less satisfying than was experienced by the first generation of retirees. Yes, you must get serious and do the work. But you can do it!

Most of the people reading this book should be able to create the retirement they desire. I know this because I know the type of people that will most likely be reading this book. They have been my students. They have been my clients. I have heard from them as grateful retirees. I have appreciated their gratitude for the information I provided, for the education they almost never got, and for the better decisions they made as a result.

Retirement is an opportunity. It is an opportunity to do things you never had the time for during your working years. It is a chance to plan how to spend your next 20, 25, or even 30-plus years. I say *bolder, not older.* But to take advantage of the retirement opportunity, you must plan and prepare. Most of all, you need to know the new rules of retirement planning.

In coming chapters, we'll look at how to estimate retirement spending, and how to make the most of what you have accumulated for retirement. You'll learn how to invest in the five to ten years leading up to retirement and during retirement. (Hint: Not by taking more risk.)

I think you know by now that I am not going to give you the same stale old advice most people hear. It is advice that is not working too well; "start early," "invest the maximum in a 401(k) account," "more bonds as you get older," and "you're in it for the long haul." Think of this book as your instruction manual for the new world of retirement. You can have the retirement you desire, but you must act now to stay ahead of the dramatic and rapid changes taking place. You must understand that 'hope' is not a plan. For those who are already retired, looking closely at your plan now and not later is even more important. Does the plan you have in place provide the confidence and certainty you want? Those who neglect to learn about the shifting world of retirement fill their retirement years with worry and anxiety. Those who understand the new rules of retirement will make decisions with confidence, taking advantage of all their retirement opportunities.

Chapter 1
Takeaways

- Science and medical care allow us to live longer. That means our money must last longer too.
- The days of the pension are gone, for the most part. We must figure out how to create income we can count on, using the new rules and the new tools.
- Inflation is a silent killer. You will never see inflation loss on your savings account or CD statements. But the loss is real. Inflation can halve your spending power over a 25-year retirement—at a time when you will need to double it!
- Anyone thinking they can live safely and with confidence out of a portfolio of volatile assets may have a very unpleasant awakening—and when it is too late to do anything about it. You must not get into a position where you have to spend or live on money from your portfolio that has gone down in value due to market risk and volatility. That is a big no-no!
- In one regard, and maybe one regard only, retirement is like any stage of life. It has a lot to do with what we make of it. Figure out how to live a secure and low-stress life, and be bold. Retirement is not for the weak of heart.

"To be yourself in a world that is constantly trying to make you something else is the greatest accomplishment."

—Ralph Waldo Emerson—

Chapter 2

Retirement Planning is 'spending' Planning

As the local chapter president for the American Financial Education Alliance, a 501(c)3, non-profit educational company dedicated to financial literacy, I teach retirement courses to 55-and-uppers at the local community college and retirement relevant workshops at the library near my home in Southern California. When I first tell student attendees, "The main goal of a retirement plan is *to 'be sure' you have enough income to maintain your retirement standard of living for* the rest of your life," they are typically thrown off. I can see it in their expressions. They explain that they "thought," that they had "heard" from 'someone' else (the media, the TV talking heads, even their advisor), that the goal was to *continue to grow their money* for later years.

I know, therefore, that many of you are hearing this for the first time too. That was one of my main goals for writing the book; to let more people know retirement planning is *spending* planning. Consider yourself lucky to be hearing it. Even if you do not agree in the end, at least you have another perspective to factor into your future decisions. At worst, you have been warned. I repeat, "Retirement planning is *spending* planning." Most people will never hear this information, and therefore they will not have the opportunity to take advantage of new and different strategies. You do.

Okay, spending. You first need to estimate how much your standard of living will cost per year. Then you begin to figure out how *you* will generate the *specific* income needed to provide for your particular lifestyle. We are all different. (I cannot say this enough.) Your plan must be about you, about your lifestyle. Once you learn how to estimate your future needs, we will consider ways to provide that income in the next chapter.

It is not easy to make retirement plans, but it is easier than many people think. It starts with how much income you will need when you retire and forever thereafter. You cannot even safely decide on a retirement date without estimating the cost of your retirement. Every other part of your retirement plan hinges on how much you intend and can afford to spend. I repeat, the plan must start with how much income you will need. If that figure is off a little, the rest of your plan will be off a little. If it is off a lot, your plan will be off a lot. The steps we discuss in this chapter will give you a good handle on how long your money is likely to last under your current practices and let you know if any adjustments need to be made. Once you have your required spending needs dialed in, it is a good idea—even necessary—to repeat the exercise every year or so after you retire. If any adjustments need to be made, it is best to know and to make them sooner than later. If this is something your current advisor does not do on an annual basis, find someone else.

This is an immensely important exercise. Your retirement security depends on it. We all know the greatest fear of most Americans approaching, or in retirement is *not having enough income and assets* to last through retirement. Even super-wealthy people have concerns about their standard of living eroding in retirement. Ask anyone retired for five years or more and you are likely to hear, "We didn't do a good enough job of estimating retirement spending." Estimating your retirement spending—even if you are off and need to adjust—puts you at a huge advantage versus doing nothing. People who exert effort to estimate their expenses and income needs create an opportunity to better their position in retirement. Your *rate of spending* has as much to do with a successful plan as *rate of growth*—maybe more. When it comes to income planning, stale and oversimplified old rules are harmful. Living longer with less certainty from pensions and Social Security means you must use a better and more accurate way to estimate your retirement spending and income needs. Rules of thumb reflect averages and may not provide the best information. You don't need what the "average person" needs. You need what you need for the life you intend to live, right?

Earlier I mentioned a TIAA-CREF study that found many people expected to need 25–75% of their working income once retired. What?! If that is "thinking," it is wishful thinking. The most common rule of thumb, as I stated earlier, is the "80% Rule." This rule assumes that retirement spending will be in the range of 65–85% of pre-retirement income. Most often I hear financial professionals recommending 80%. Why? Because you won't be paying into Social Security any longer. You will not be commuting. Supposedly your clothing expense should be less. You will not be contributing to your retirement plan. Lunches will more often be eaten at home rather than out.

That seems sensible. What I see in my practice, however, is that eliminated expenses will be replaced by other, sometimes unexpected expenses and spending. Your retirement lifestyle will evolve. What will you do in retirement? Will it require a lot of spending or a little? Retirement spending is unique for each person or household, so you should not use averages and rules of thumb as your final answer. Sometimes expenses increase in retirement, especially in the early years. The higher your pre-retirement income, the more likely it is that you will spend the same or more. As a Retirement Income Certified Professional doing income planning... for life, I rarely see the flip side, with people who spend considerably less in retirement than when they were working. Not in Southern California, at least.

In addition to the 80% rule of thumb, the Double Trouble Method is another widely used method for estimating retirement financial needs. It is a very simple way to estimate spending, which explains part of the appeal, as it is simple. Many Wall Street advisor types who want you to keep your money at risk (just like during your working years) espouse this 'simplified' method. Sometimes this method is called the *ballpark method* because it gives a spending need amount that is less than accurate. But hey, at least it is in the ballpark. Good enough, right? Wrong! I do not like this method for that reason. And more importantly, I do not like it because this method uses "hypothetical" returns to provide income. Your spending is not hypothetical, your life is not hypothetical—it is real. Most retirees find more security and peace of mind *knowing* the money they need is going to be there versus "hypothetically" be there. What do you think? I will not expound on the Double Trouble Method more here. If you are curious you can learn more about it online.

All other simple rules to estimate retirement spending have shortcomings. So let's throw out the general rules. We can use rules of thumb and income replacement ratios for conversation and education, but I do not recommend them to estimate your retirement spending needs. Developing a spending estimate that fits your specific lifestyle goals will serve you much better.

Keep in mind that retirement planning is about more than finances—a lot more. You need to give some thought to the kind of life you intend to live in retirement, followed by an estimate of what that would cost in today's dollars, tomorrow and beyond. You'll have daily activities, as well as weekly, monthly, and less frequent activities. You'll have regular necessary expenses for food, shelter, utilities, and medical care. There will be periodic necessary expenses such as replacing cars and household items. Some people refer to this approach as *life planning* or *holistic expense planning*. Call it whatever you want. The important thing is that the activities you engage in will determine your specific spending needs. This kind of homework and pre-planning will reduce your likelihood of running out of money in retirement if you spend your nest egg too rapidly. Studies have shown that those who are most satisfied and financially secure in retirement are those who made the time to do pre-retirement planning, and most importantly, those who understood that retirement planning is income planning. It only makes sense, right? We live on 'regular' and steady, dependable income during the working years. It should be no surprise that the same works well for the retirement years too. Many 'plans' have retirees deciding how much they can spend each year, based on what their nest egg did last year, and how it performed based on 'the market'. Not my idea of fun, not my idea of a good plan.

Once you have carefully thought through your desired retirement lifestyle and have estimated the initial cost, you will feel much better. You will have taken the necessary and first big step to a secure retirement future. Your spending plan will have expenses that can be put into several categories. There are the essentials: food, housing, medical insurance, and so on. Then there are *wants*, and beyond those, *extra* things we would like to do in our ideal retirement life. (That's your "bucket list.") For some people, there is a fourth level; legacy. This does not always mean leaving money after you are gone. It can also be a way to designate funds to help others while you are still living; such as giving money to a favorite charity, or to your children and grandchildren.

Keep in mind that these categories do not need to be too rigid. Some spending may overlap. For instance, some clothing is a necessary expense. Other apparel may be in the "like to have" category. Hamburger may be in the basic category, filet mignon in the "like to have" category. If you golf, then golfing on a public course may be in your basic category, while Pebble Beach is in the "nice to do" category. For someone else the public course may be "nice to do" and Pebble Beach the "bucket list." This is *your* retirement, *your* assets, *your* future ... *your plan*.

It is not uncommon for pre-retirees to find that all of these expenses are too much for their resources the first time around. You must be realistic. A plan that will work balances a lifestyle you will enjoy living, with the income you will have available to fund it. It may require a redo or two, but in the end, you will have an accurate dollar amount for your income requirement or goal. Again, that is where it all starts.

Once you have estimated your first-year retirement income needs, you need to estimate the length of retirement. Keep in mind it is always better to plan to live longer and have the money you need than to plan for a shorter life span and thus come up short when you live beyond that planned age. You don't want to find yourself in a situation where your money is gone and you're still around. That will impact your dignity and independence.

You need to make a psychological switch. You have always been told something along the lines of, "Figure out the retirement life you want to live, how much it will take and set about saving and growing enough money to fund it all." Unfortunately, even into the retirement years, many people are lead to believe that retirement is about growth and trying to get bigger returns. Now you need to understand; in retirement, your *growth years* are behind you; once you are finished working, you are in the *spending years.* In terms of financial goals, asset growth should be second to proper retirement asset allocation—asset allocation designed for maximum *income* rather than maximum *growth*. It is time to understand that what you were taught was either backwards, or at least no longer useful, now that you are closing in on retirement. It is best to think in terms of, "Okay, this is the money we have, how can we make the most of it? What kind of life can we live... on it? Even, "Where can we live, on it?" sometimes. You hopefully see the difference. The former always has you stressing, thinking, "We need more." It has you taking a risk to get more. The latter allows us to deal with reality, and make the most of what we have. It teaches us that growth is necessary to keep up with inflation, to maintain the spending power we have, not shoot for, and hope for more. There is great peace in the acceptance of reality, and going about making the most of that.

We must address the most widely used method of determining the likelihood that you will have enough money for the rest of your life. This method of estimating the "odds" utilizes *Monte Carlo simulations.* You might be wondering why the method used by most financial advisors to determine the chances of running out of money in retirement is named after the gambling mecca of Monte Carlo? Well, here is the explanation from Investopedia; *Monte Carlo simulations are named after the gambling hot spot in Monaco, since chance and random outcomes are central to the modeling technique, much as they are to games like roulette, dice, and slot machines. Stanislaw Ulam, a mathematician who worked on the Manhattan Project, first developed the technique.* The method attempts, via many different possible outcomes, to answer the question, "What are the chances I will run out of money?" It is a *range* of possibilities not suited for 55-and-uppers who prefer more certainty.

For many years prior to modern computing capabilities and these simulations, "safe" rates of return were calculated using an annual average rate of return. This is known as a linear or **deterministic model.** The problem is that the market does not return "averages"—it fluctuates. Oh, and you will learn later in this book that you do not earn 'average rates' of return. You earn *real rates* of return. Oftentimes those are two quite different numbers. You are sold investments using "averages" and then you earn *real* rates. Hmmm…

is it just me, or does this sound deceptive? Though this is common practice, I consider it misleading at best. The average rates of return fluctuate dramatically. Imagine an income plan anticipating a 7% annual return, using Monte Carlo simulations, which is not uncommon. You need money out of that account to live on, you plan to take money out of that account, and then suddenly it drops 20%. That is an exercise in futility. False security. Meaningless even. Also, it is very important to know, while most financial professionals are putting a plan together for you, built around average rates of return, you MUST live on the real rate of return you actually get, in your specific portfolio. Can we all say together, Y I K E S! Really, do you not think this is something everyone nearing retirement should be aware of?

With modern computing capabilities, along comes the ability to "simulate" portfolio performance using as many as 500 different market-performance periods in history (rather than averages). This is known as the **probabilistic model** and was not used very much until the early 2000s. It is definitely better than the deterministic model, but again, it's called the "Monte Carlo method" for a reason. It merely provides many possible outcomes, using many different returns as possibilities. There is a range of certainty that the market will perform within the parameters—and that range is never 100%. The program determines the percentage of times the investment capital (your retirement money) lasts for the entire retirement period. That is the probability the plan will be successful. The goal is to get the portfolio into a range of 'only' 10–15% chance of failure; that is considered "good enough." Let me ask you something. If it turns out you end up in the 15% that did not work, do you care that your portfolio had an 85% possibility of success? No! When assumptions used for input are exaggerated and /or inaccurate, the outcomes can be flawed as well as just a guess. Another issue I have with this method is that "failure" is not defined. It could be failure by a few months and a few dollars, or failure by many years and many dollars.

This strategy seems weak at best and not reassuring at all. I mean, there is only a 0.8%, less than 1% chance that my house will burn down. But I still have insurance just in case I am in that 0.8%.

What about you? If you get on a plane and the pilot says you have an 85% chance of landing safely, how long will it take you to reach the exit door? Providing sufficient money to live on for the rest of your life is at least as important as your plane landing safely. At least if your plane does not land safely, it will be over quickly and you won't need to worry about running out of money. (It was a joke.)

Here's one more problem. This method assumes you follow the plan for the entire rest of your life, no matter what comes. That is unrealistic. That is not what people do, nor what advisors do, with your money. Advisors make changes to the portfolio based on market fluctuations and various other factors, including their income. A retiree may make changes based on how their retirement life unfolds and evolves. Now the simulations that your "plan" was built upon are mostly useless and the exercise was for nothing. Can you spell p-r-o-b-l-e-m?

I want to end this chapter by assuring you there is a better way to plan income for the remainder of your life. It is a method that builds in guarantees that provide the certainty you need to be comfortable. It provides the peace of mind that you can only get from *knowing* what your income will be. After all, retirement is supposed to be the best of the rest of your life. You do not want worry about how you are going to eat, or how you are going to shrink your lifestyle year after year to fit your ever-decreasing spending power. Remember; *retirement planning is spending planning.*

Retirement is all about the income. I repeat, it's all about the income. You may get sick of hearing this, but it seems that almost everyone—retirees, pre-retirees, and even financial professionals—are distracted and focused on the wrong things. They all-too-often have priorities out of order. The most important goal for 55-and-uppers, should be *establishing a steady and secure income stream for their retirement years.* This income stream will provide them the degree of certainty they desire, based on reality. I did not say, 'the degree of certainty that their advisor desires is okay with'. This is *your* retirement, *your* money and *your* life. It will suffer if this most important piece of your retirement planning is poorly executed. To be absolutely 100% clear, the goal is to allocate your assets in a way that makes sure they last as long as you last. The goal is *income—*

sufficient income that will allow you to maintain your independence and dignity for the rest of your life.

It was easier for our parents and grandparents. Social Security and pensions were dependable. Our predecessors also had risk-free CDs, treasury bonds, and other decent interest-earning investments. Interest rates were higher for them. But since it looks like we may have Japanese-style low, and possibly even negative interest rates for years to come, these options are no longer available for us. Oh, and don't forget that we are expected to live longer too.

(Please excuse me if I remind you of some principles and information multiple times in this book. It is intentional. In this one little book I am trying to counter maybe thirty-plus years of what you have learned, of what you think you "know." Reminders are necessary.)

Unless you have a lot more money than you are going to need—and I mean a *lot*—today's interest rates will not allow the strategies our parents and grandparents employed. Those options pay way less than inflation today, which means you are locking in loss of spending power each year. That is a non-starter for most of your assets. You need your assets working for you to keep up with inflation.

As our political scene continues to evolve, debt is likely to spiral ever higher. Program adjustments will require us to cover things our parents had covered on their behalf by Social Security, Medicare, or company-provided retirement benefits. These are becoming unknown to us, and may become totally unknown during our retirement years.

Think of your plan as the roadmap for your financial future. If you were planning a trip across the country, you would map out desired sights and stops along the way. Planning your retirement journey also needs to be mapped out. On a long, multi-week cross-country trip many things can happen that you did not expect. Maybe a storm causes road damage and you need to reroute. Maybe the hotel or campground you were going to stay at is closed unexpectedly. Maybe you decide halfway across the country to stop and visit an old friend you just realized lives 40 miles off your route. Unexpected things come up on trips, right? Having flexibility and options when on a trip are is important too, right? Especially when you are no longer on a work schedule.

The retirement journey is very similar. You put the map together based on all the best information: your goals, objectives, and resources, along with your likely and intended lifestyle. As you travel your retirement path, life will happen—just like on the cross-country trip. Unanticipated things will happen and you will need to adjust. Therefore, your retirement plan should have flexibility built in. Maybe a detour is necessary, but then you can get back on track, following the map and the income plan you put into place for your retirement journey. To maintain the sense of security that comes from a dependable income plan, you need to review the plan regularly—at least annually. It is not a set-it-and-forget-it plan.

As you set up this plan, you will be prioritizing your spending. Remember? Basic needs come first, then wants, then extras (the "bucket list"), then legacy. Step one to the right income plan is thinking about what you will do, then estimating and prioritizing your retirement spending.

The next step is building a solid retirement foundation. At least for the basics, you want your sources of income to be guaranteed: pension(s), Social Security, rental income, cash value life insurance, inheritance, annuities, and the like. Let me repeat: *Guaranteed* sources work best for essential needs. Without having the basics guaranteed, retirement will be very stressful. In both the United States and the United Kingdom, it has been shown that retirement satisfaction is significantly greater when basic needs are guaranteed and retirees do not have to worry about them. Lower stress also means more enjoyment and often a longer life.

Aside from guaranteeing your basic needs, every 'other' method of income planning leaves you *hoping* versus *knowing* how your basic needs will be provided. Every time the market hiccups, you get nervous. When it takes a drop, you are mentally reevaluating, adjusting, asking "Are we going to be okay?" Large drops, even for relatively short periods, cause worry to set in. You wonder if you will run out of money. Emotionally motivated, poor financial decisions can then often occur, compounding the problem.

When your paycheck ceases and the rest of your life depends

on your current assets, market fluctuations can cause panic, abrupt spending, and lifestyle changes. Once this happens it is very difficult to get back on track—a lower lifestyle quickly becomes the norm. I have seen too many unfortunate retirees' lives changed for the worse because of the 2000 and 2008 market drops, along with the poor decisions and bearish years that followed. Some retirees were forced to sell and move to a less expensive area, downsize, scramble for a job, take in room renters, or move in with family. These are real-life situations.

I could go into more detail, but I think you get the point. You must have *some* money to live on, and money to spend that has not gone down in value. That requires *principal protection*. Once you have established sufficient income guarantees in line with your likely lifetime needs, you can have more peace of mind about the risk you take with other assets.

Chapter 2
Takeaways

- We don't know what we don't know... until we know. New information allows us to see things in a different light, analyze what we are doing, and decide to continue or change.
- Once we reach retirement, the earning years are over. The spending years begin. This requires a different strategy than the strategy we used to save for retirement.
- Our planning became more difficult when the banks, Uncle Sam, and Wall Street decided it was better for 'them' to eliminate pensions and get baby boomers (no apostrophe) to put trillions of dollars into the stock market—a game they don't know how to play.
- When you take more risk than you can afford, you are literally putting your retirement lifestyle in jeopardy. Losses in retirement—big losses like in 2008—will cause the rest of your life to be financially diminished. Even small loses will cause you to rethink your day-to-day life.

"Annual income twenty pounds, annual expenditure nineteen six, result happiness. Annual income twenty pounds, annual expenditure twenty pound ought and six, result misery."

—Charles Dickens in *David Copperfield*—

Chapter 3

Get Your Assets Together

Some of the income sources to be considered and utilized when planning for a lifetime of spending and post-career cash flow include but are not limited to; Social Security, any pensions available, distribution or spending strategies utilizing your nest egg assets, growth strategies for nest egg assets, annuities, strategies that can decrease or minimize taxes, rental income, room rental, potential inheritance, trust deed or other income from money loaned, etcetera.

Now the challenge is to figure out how to meet your needs. Are you okay with guessing and hoping where your retirement income will come from? Or do you want to *know*? Fifty-five-and-uppers are all wondering the same thing. Will my Social Security, my savings, my 401(k), my IRA, and other retirement assets be enough? Is there a way to do anything other than "hope so"?

A couple I recently helped came into my office feeling like they were in the dark. They both had decent Social Security benefits, but neither really knew when to file or how much their monthly checks would be. Brian had a modest pension from a previous employer, assuming he would start it at age 66. He also had a 401(k) from the same previous employer, as well as an IRA he had been adding to over the years. He had nothing from his current employer as he had only been there for three years. He was hoping to retire at age 65 with Darlene, his spouse of many years. Darlene had a 401(k), and together they had some money in savings and mutual funds. Their issue was that they had no idea how to convert what they had worked for all these years into income to live on.

Brian and Darlene are not alone feeling like they are in the dark about their retirement. The truth is that many of the students who attend my courses on safe money planning—and probably many people reading this book—feel much the same. They worked hard to get to where they are and they have some assets. But they have no idea how to get from the paychecks of the working years to *retirement income certainty.*

Most people do not even know if they will need more or less money in retirement. I have heard of the early retirement years referred to as the go-go years, the middle years as the slow-slow years, and the last years as the no-no years. Even so, that does not tell you which years you are likely to need more income!

Even with the best-made and best-executed plans, life often happens in ways we not expect. I know of a 68- and 69-year-old couple that were at dinner with friends, received a phone call, and within two hours were effectively parents to their 1-year-old grandson. Life happens. For decades, you work hard and save for retirement. You hope the money you have the day you retire will be enough. The question is this; is *hope* what you want to build your retirement upon? I mean, do you want to spend what you intend to be the best, most peaceful, and most enjoyable part of your entire life hoping you will have sufficient income?

Hope is not a plan. And it should not be the way people spend their retirement years. The two options, *Hoping* for a happy ending versus *Knowing* with certainty are worlds apart. The good news is that with education, information, the proper tools, and the right financial professional guidance, a successful retirement strategy is possible. This plan will incorporate sufficient guarantees for [your] personal situation, ensuring your security and peace of mind as you manage your financial life in retirement.

The fortunate pre-retirees I typically get to meet in my courses have Social Security benefits along with a nest egg of 401(k), IRA, and other assets. But they do not understand their financial big picture, nor do they know what to do with the assets they have accumulated to make them last. Saving and investing for retirement during the working years is one thing. Putting together a retirement plan to create an income-generating retirement that *mimics* the working years requires a different approach.

Both the working years and the retirement years are important. If you have accumulated a nest egg of assets for retirement, then you are to be commended. That said, you are only on the 50-yard line, and it is only halftime. The second half of your retirement game 'strategy' is what you will count on to get you over the goal line. Or, it will cause you to lose the game with insufficient income to maintain your independence and dignity. On top of market volatility, low interest rates, and inflation, there are the issues of taxes, required minimum distributions (RMDs) from qualified plans, legacy planning, and healthcare. These are all 'second-half issues'. You can see that safely crossing that goal line will take more than hope. How can you play the second half well? With a well-thought-out and well-executed plan, focused on the income you need in retirement. This is not only my professional opinion, but also what I see played out every day with my clients. Those retirees 'hoping' are nervous; those that 'know' seem more relaxed.

So here you are on the 50-yard line of your financial life. What's your plan? Knowing that you will start Social Security benefits at some point, knowing you have other assets you will draw from, it is time to huddle up and put together a plan. A plan that will significantly impact not only how much money you get to live on, but also how much peace of mind you get to enjoy once you punch the clock for the last time. With the help of the right financial professional, you need to put a plan into action that deals with risk management, *real* asset diversification, tax planning, and income planning for the rest of your life. The right strategy for you will be one that allows you to achieve the maximum benefit from each one of the hard-earned dollars you have set aside for your retirement.

Advice about what to do with your money has been around for as long as money has been around. Reviewing the last thirty years, we can see what has worked and what has not. The last ten years shed even better light on the subject. Only a few investment concepts have stood even this short test of time. Strategies for retirees should not be built upon always-changing market conditions, swings in the economy, and conditions around the world.

Doing the same thing over and over again and expecting different results ... makes no sense. Just ask Albert Einstein, right? Investment strategies, savings plans, and retirement strategies that worked in the past have collided with a whole new world of complicated market and political circumstances, new legislation, uncertain tax questions and more. These circumstances have caused old strategies to be ineffective at the most important time of your financial life... retirement. The huge recession of the early 2000's and the financial debacle of 2008 showed all too many hardworking retirees that old investment ideas were not only ineffective, but frighteningly destructive to their retirement plans. The completely restructured, currently unknown nature of our future health care system brings with it new challenges that will undoubtedly change how we plan for healthcare, as well as how insurance companies provide investment retirement products and services. Moreover, we are living longer. New actuarial tables are out and will affect Social Security. They will also change how much guaranteed lifetime income insurance companies provide.

The biggest, most painful lesson retirees got from the Great Recession is this: If you are not sufficiently involved with your money, or lack the understanding about what your money is invested in or why, and are not able to grasp the full potential of the risks involved. In such a case, it is unlikely that things will end well. A lack of real knowledge about risk will work against you, potentially take away your chance of security, erode your peace of mind, and change your plans for retirement—as well as your legacy. Continuing to do what you have always done is not the best way to make the most of what you have. You must establish a solid and sensible approach to managing your assets for the last decades of life.

Managing your money, income, and investments is an ongoing process. To be as successful as possible, you will require the right professional help. If your plan is set up well from the outset, flexibility and adapting to a changing world will be easier and financially speaking, less risky. Twice-yearly, or sometimes just annual meetings with your advisor will be sufficient as long as you create the plan together, understanding your risk tolerance. Then you will be able to sleep at night no matter what happens in the markets.

I cannot state it enough; the retirement front is changing and will continue to do so. What worked for our parents or even our parents' parents may have been okay for them back then. But 55-and-uppers approaching retirement or people already retired today must make use of new ideas, new strategies, new tools, and the 'right' professional guidance.

Hope or Know ... Up to You

Many advisors unintentionally make retirement planning more complicated than necessary. See, when it comes to retirement, there are only two *types of money* you need to think about. All your money will fall into one of two categories. There is money you *know* will be there for you when you need or want it ... and then there is money you *hope* will be there when you need it or want it. You must determine how much of each type of money will provide you with the most peace of mind.

"Hope So" money is money subject to market loss. It will go up and down with the market. Though market-based assets have always gone up *over time,* there is no guarantee how little or how much your assets will be worth *at any given time.* The value is affected by market volatility, investor activity, your decisions, and your advisors' decisions. 'Hope So' money rises and falls based on market trends, investment fads, buying trends, politics, the economy, short and long term rates, taxes, unemployment, weather, and more. You get the point.

You have probably heard, that as your money is exposed to more risk, it also has the potential for more reward. The key word here is "potential." There is absolutely no evidence that more risk taken with all your assets will always mean better growth and more assets later. Actually, a good bit of evidence indicates that a truly diversified portfolio of retirement assets—some at risk and some protected—is much more likely to provide better growth. Furthermore, principal protected investments provide something even more important, something most retirees' want: protection. That means money to live on when they need it.

Retirees, who understand this, balance their assets between 'Hope So' and 'Know So' money. Thus, they tend to sleep much better at night. Since the market is volatile and subject to change, you cannot be sure what the value of your investments will be in the future. You cannot rely on it with any degree of certainty. For this reason, we refer to it as 'Hope So' money. This doesn't mean you should have zero money invested in the market—but it would be dangerous to assume you can know what it will be worth at any given point in the future. Yes, if the market does what it has always done, your money will be worth more at some later point. The problem is that it will also be worth less at some points—and we don't know when or how much. These unknowns pose a real problem for retirees planning for the income they need.

"Hope So" money is the money retirees can afford to risk with the "hope" of higher returns. This is appropriate for money earmarked for a longer investment timeframe. This may be right for the money you are leaving to others. Some retirees think of this money as their money for extras: that big vacation, a new car, helping kids, and the like. Think of it as money that will not affect your day-to-day lifestyle if you lose it. Over the long run, time can smooth out the highs and lows of money exposed to the market. But depending on 'Hope So' money for daily needs and living expenses is not wise. Why? Because the money fluctuates. Spending money that has gone down in value is a huge mistake. Think about it. Say you had invested two dollars in 2008 and lost one to market volatility. Then you withdrew and spent the one-dollar you had left. You really spent two dollars that you will never get back. And those two dollars would have been $5.33 in 25 years at a 4% compounded growth rate. That is $5.33 you will never see, $5.33 you were likely counting on for your inflation-adjusted income.

"Know So" money, on the other hand, provides certainty. This is money that you can count on; money that you *know* will be there for you. 'Know So' money consists of dependable, principal-protected assets. Social Security is one source of 'Know So' money for most retirees. The income from Social Security is guaranteed. You have paid into Social Security your entire working life, and you can rely on that stream of income during your retirement. For many it is the only pension-like money they will have. Unfortunately, Social Security only provides for about 40% of the average retiree's household budget. The key for a successful, less-stressful retirement for many is to add to their pension-like income. (I am sure some of you are thinking; Social Security may not be dependable for much longer. This will be looked at in another chapter, along with how to gain peace of mind about Social Security dependability. The lesson to be learned here is that the retirement years require a different way of thinking about *security* than your working years did. In the retirement years, security means certainty—and certainty in the form of more steady income, not just more dollars.

Studies conducted in England and the United States have found that people who have more guaranteed, pension-like income are happier, they worry less and even live longer.[1] Unlike 'Hope So' money, 'Know So' money may not be as exciting, but that is the point. In my practice, I have found that one thing most retirees *do not want* when it comes to their hard-earned nest egg money is "excitement." 'Know So' money may be boring to some people, but it is safe. You can provide some excitement with the income.

Ideally, you can balance an acceptable rate of risk with the right amount of guarantees to suit your situation, needs, and desires. Historically, there have been times when interest rates were higher and market volatility was lower. During those 'times' you can save money in the bank and get a decent return. You could invest in the market and likely be successful with a wide range of options. During those times, you could have chosen risky or protected investments and done okay either way. It was difficult to make a mistake. But it is always easier to look back and see what would have worked better. Looking forward, not so much! Today, retirees don't have the benefit of calmer markets and higher savings rates. Market volatility is at all-time highs, while interest rates are at all-time lows. And it might be this way for many years. We do not know.

The retirement plan most readers have in place is the plan that was put in place to *accumulate money during the working years.* That plan is to save money (typically in a 401(k), IRA, etcetera), invest that money in stocks, bonds, and mutual funds (usually with very little knowledge), and... hope for the best. Are you reading this at a time when the markets are up? If so, you are fortunate (lucky).

---

1. http://business.time.com/2012/07/30/lifetime-income-stream-key-to-retirement-happiness/;
https://blogs.wsj.com/experts/2013/10/31/happiness-in-retirement-is-a-steady-income/

You have some money. But how long will it last? This plan for accumulating money may not only prevent you from achieving your retirement goals—it may also irreparably harm you. We only get one chance to plan retirement right. You will not be able to wake up one day in your late 70s with maybe another 20 years of life to live, out of money, and say, "Well, that didn't work out too well. Let's try it again." Restarting is not possible. Currently, the rates for most safe investment options are low, and the volatility of 'Hope So' money is higher than ever. Few overlapping saving and investment options can provide what retirees need; protection and money that keeps pace with inflation. Because of this uncertain financial landscape, wise investment strategies are more important now than ever. As baby boomers, our unique situation requires fresh ideas and investment tools—ones most people are not even aware of. Today, you need a different plan: A plan that will work and one you can count on.

Most 55-and-uppers don't know how much risk they are exposed to. You must organize your assets so you can have a clear understanding of where your money is invested. You need to know how much risk your nest egg assets are exposed to versus how much of your assets are in safer, protected investment and savings vehicles. This process starts with listing what all your assets are.

'Hope So' Money Versus 'Know So' Money

'Hope So' money is the money that you *hope* will be there when you need it. 'Hope So' money counts on your luck holding out and the economy holding up. It depends on the buying and selling of risk type investments at the right time. It counts on the financial winds blowing favorably upon you. Some examples of 'Hope So' money include:
- Market mutual funds, including index funds, equity funds, bond funds, balanced funds, target date funds, exchange traded funds (ETFs), etc.
- Variable annuities
- Variable life insurance
- Real Estate Investment Trusts

- Master Limited Partnerships
- Hedge funds
- Managed accounts
- Trust deed investing

On the other hand, there is money that you are confident will always be there when you need it. This 'Know So' money is money you can count on. It is protected money, not exposed to market volatility and therefore not subject to downside losses. Sources of 'Know So' money include:

- Social Security
- Pensions
- U. S. Government backed securities and bonds
- Savings and checking accounts
- Fixed income annuities
- Fixed indexed life insurance
- CDs
- Treasuries
- Money market accounts
- MYGAs or Mutli-Year Guaranteed Annuities

Dean and Barb had worked hard and saved diligently for their retirement years. They attended a safe money course I teach at a local community college. Like most retirees and soon-to-be-retirees, they had the majority of their nest egg assets in the market. Their nest egg was invested in 'Hope So' investments. Barb was retired, and Dean was very near retirement. After attending my course and gaining some new insights, they intuitively knew the time had come to shift some of their hard-earned assets so they were principal-protected. They wanted to be sure it would always be there. But what vehicle should they use? And how much money should they move from risk to protected?

The Rule of 100

It is very important for you to figure out how much risk is right for you in your specific situation. You must realistically understand the amount of assets you have to live on. You must understand how long those assets will last. Compounding the retirement planning that is necessary, the question of risk, and the likely best asset allocation are all the variables inherent in everyone's individual situation. No two situations are the same. Feeling comfortable with where and how your nest egg assets are invested is your most important financial decision. Education is the key to understanding. You do not want worry to be the biggest part of your golden years, right?

Your financial professional is supposed to help you make decisions that align your money with who you are, with how you plan to live in retirement, and (most importantly) with your risk tolerance criteria. That includes how you feel when you lose hard-earned assets. And more importantly, it includes the ability of your nest egg to take the hit of inevitable market losses without forcing you to dial back your standard of living, reduce your lifestyle and cut back on or eliminate things you want to do.

A few hurdles prevent most financial professionals from doing what they are supposed to do on your behalf, in this regard. One is, most financial professionals do not make available *truly balanced portfolios.* My definition of "balanced" is balanced between *risk* and *no risk* (not high risk and less risk). This should be your definition of "balanced" too; some money protected against loss and some at risk. Though you hopefully have many eggs in your retirement basket, they are probably all in the same Wall Street basket. Remember 2008? All of those eggs lost value. Risk-type investments all have one thing in common... risk. Go figure. Most financial professionals earn their money only when your assets are at risk in the Wall Street stock-market basket. If they were to recommend that you, as a retiree or near-retiree hold some of your assets anywhere else, that would impact them financially. Their paycheck would take a hit. Most are more concerned about their paycheck taking a hit than they are your nest egg taking a hit. Sad but true.

Financial professionals, who recommend only risk-type investments, allowing no room for principal-protected investments, create a conflict between what retirees need and what they offer. Here is the reality of retirement finance; the two things most retirees need and want for their assets are *protection and growth without risk.* Yes, I said growth without risk. For some of your assets, moderate or even low growth makes a lot more sense than *loss*. Regarding your nest egg assets, they will need to provide the additional income you will need to fill in the gaps not provided by Social Security and pensions. Remember, once your earning years are over, your financial life is about spending, about *income*, about how you will pay yourself for the rest of your life.

The second issue that prevents many financial professionals from doing the right thing on your behalf is that most financial professionals have never even heard of, let alone studied or understood, Modern Retirement Theory (MRT). They are all using Modern Portfolio Theory (MPT) to manage your accounts. Modern Portfolio Theory was never intended nor developed for (you). It was never meant to be used for the management of (your) money—not even during the working years, let alone in retirement. Yet that is what is happening. (We will learn much more about this in a later chapter.)

Another reason your retirement future may be at risk is that most financial professionals are employees. They work for a company. The company's number one goal is *profit*. Therefore, as employees, most financial professionals are obligated to do what the employer wants them to do; make money for the company.

Remember how I said my financial career began as a stockbroker? Remember how I said I was naïve? I recall the disturbing day my supervisor told me, "As stockbrokers we get paid to sell stocks, bonds and mutual funds. It is our goal and mission to make money whether the market goes up, or the market goes down. We do not intentionally want to harm anyone, but ... hey, sometimes people get hurt." Yikes! And to think this is the cavalier attitude still being 'perpetrated' upon hardworking, unsuspecting, hopeful people today. I am upset by the all-too-often dishonest status quo of typical financial advice. But I'll conclude that discussion for now. We need to talk about the Rule of 100.

When you ask questions like: What kind of life do I intend to live in retirement? How much money do I need to live that life? When will I need to begin using (spending) some of the money I have saved over my lifetime? That is *Income Planning*. Income planning is a very specific niche of financial planning—another niche most financial professionals have never studied and therefore know little about.

In retirement, your income causes you to succeed or to lose your independence and dignity. Managing your risk by balancing 'Hope So' money with 'Know So' money will stack the deck in favor of a happier, less stressful, more certain retirement. It is the first step to *true* retirement planning (i.e., income planning). Everything else in this book follows this foundation, one of a *truly diversified asset allocation* model. The 'Know So' / 'Hope So' asset allocation model is not a strategy but *the* strategy; it rescues some of your retirement eggs from the risk basket and protects them to ensure you always have money to live on (money that has not gone down in value). The question is this; how much of your assets should be used to secure your income needs for the rest of your life? Once you know the answer, the issue of how much 'Hope So' money you should keep at risk will be much easier to resolve.

Some risk is prudent for most retirees because, while 'Know So' money is protected, safe, and dependable, 'Know So' investments work differently. For true diversification, as I stated previously, you need some protected assets and some risk assets. Being careful to dial in the right amount of risk for your assets and the life you want to live is important. The differing characteristics of risk investments and non-risk investments will provide the best potential for most retirees. Again, there are exceptions to almost everything. But owning some assets that never lose value due to market volatility allows you to grow from market upswings—because your assets didn't lose value on the downswing. In other words, the growth starts where it left off. Risk assets must regain their losses before you begin earning additional money with them. You might say that one way is the turtle approach and the other is the hare approach. The safer, turtle approach has the potential to earn more because it does not lose money, while the hare approach has the potential to earn more in any given year. We do not know which will work best in the short run, but the right balance for you will provide the best result over the remainder of your life. It will be a more peaceful and less-stressful ride too!

The problem to be solved is one of balance. But it is a different version of balance than what you have been taught. While there is no one-way to approach your specific investment-risk determination, there is one piece of financial advice that is universally applicable to everyone. It is the Rule of 100. The *Rule of 100* is a guideline you can use to start making decisions about your own personal and individual retirement risk management. It helps to determine your individual retirement asset allocation. The rule states that the number 100 minus a person's age equals the limit one should expose to risk (expressed in a percentage of assets). So the Rule of 100 means:

100 – [your age] = % of assets you can expose to risk

If you are a 30-year-old, the Rule of 100 indicates you could expose up to 70% of your money to risk. Your time horizon is longer, so you can use more risk-type investments. This is expressed as:

100 – [30] = 70%

Conversely, a 70-year-old, not having the same time horizon, should be exposed to less risk.

100 – [70] = 30%

You may also find it valuable to factor your "financial age" into the Rule of 100. This is different from your chronological age and varies based on your investment experience, your aversion to or acceptance of risk, and other factors such as longevity and the amount of money you have saved.

While the Rule of 100 is not the only way to determine your asset allocation, it is a very good and simple way to start. Perhaps when you are age 30 and early in your career, it makes sense to have 70% of your money in the market; time is on your side. You have plenty of time to save more money, work more, and recover from the inevitable market downturns. When you are 30, retirement is a long way off. Your earning power is likely to increase. It makes total sense that younger investors can take on more risk for exactly those reasons. The risk taken to obtain potential rewards of long-term involvement in the market is easier to justify when you are young.

However, risk tolerance decreases as you age. If you are 30 years old and lose 50% of your portfolio in a market downturn, you have many years to recover from the loss. If you are 70 years old and were planning to spend some of your money, you are now in a very different and possibly dire situation. You may not have sufficient time to recover from such loss. That would force you to break one of the biggest rules of retirement planning: You are forced to spend money that has gone down in value.

Many people are living entirely on their Social Security today because that exact scenario happened to them. They lost too much in 2008 as they retired. Then they had to live on what was left, and it disappeared all too fast. That is a retirement game changer. Most of us boomers don't like riding the roller coaster like we did when we were younger. That goes for the financial roller coaster too. There is less time to recover from downturns and the stakes are higher. The money you have saved is money you need to provide income.

Also, a large part of the benefit that comes with investing and taking risk earlier in life is related to *compounding*. Compounded earnings can be incredibly powerful over time. The longer your money has time to compound, the greater your assets will be. This is what is meant typically by "putting your money to work." This is also why the Rule of 100 favors risk for younger investors. If you start investing when you are young, you can invest smaller amounts of money in a more aggressive fashion; you have the potential to make a profit in a rising market and can harness the power of compounding earnings. As you reach the ages of 40, 50, and 60, that potential decreases. Decreasing risk as you age helps your financial wellbeing. I do not mean more bonds either! They also lost money in 2008 and are therefore just 'different' assets in the same risk basket.

Decreasing risk helps your emotional wellbeing too. Most retirees cannot emotionally tolerate the same amount of risk as they did when they were younger. Therefore, considering the Rule of 100, shifting some of your assets to protected investments is prudent.

This ensures that your hard-earned assets will provide you with the income you need in retirement.

The Rule of 100 may already be impacting your investments. Do you have a 401(k)? Many people do, but few understand how their money is allocated within their 401(k). Many 401(k) options include *target date funds* that change your risk exposure over time, essentially following a form of the Rule of 100. Selecting one of these options is meant to shift your risk and protect you as you age. This setup is a good idea that I commend, but it is often carried out poorly. Remember, most advisors are risk-only advisors. And almost all 401(k) plans are installed, maintained, and managed by risk-oriented companies.

Remember how I mentioned "balance" earlier? Risk-only type advisors and companies—the ones who earn money by advocating risk—might recommend that you put some of your assets into *less risky* investments. What's the problem? "Less risk" is still risk! This Wall Street version of the Rule of 100 failed its biggest test ever in 2008. All the "alternative" investments in the less risky portion of people's portfolios went down too! Note the use of "less risky." This is bastardizing; twisting the Rule of 100 in a deceptive manner. It puts some assets at more risk and some at less risk, but nevertheless, *all are at risk*. Forget this fact and imperil your retirement years. *True diversification* and a genuine, true use of the Rule of 100 requires you to invest the non-risk assets invested somewhere where ... there is *no* risk. Funny how that works, right?

Chapter 3
Takeaways

- There is money you *hope* you'll have in the future, and there is money you *know* you'll have in the future. Make sure you understand the difference. More importantly, know how much of each you 'need'.
- Organizing your assets starts with making a list, make an accounting of what you have, where it is invested. You can then begin to learn more so you understand how each asset is balanced to meet you goals… or not.
- Your exposure to risk is ultimately determined not by the market, not by your advisor… but by you. It's your money, it's your life, and it's your decisions that will make or break your retirement. You must know enough to be comfortable with the asset allocation decisions you make.
- Use the Rule of 100. It is an excellent and simple guiding principle. It helps you determine how much risk your retirement nest egg should be exposed to versus how much protection you should have.

*"If you believe you can, you might.
If you know you can, you will."*

—Steve Maraboli—

Chapter 4

Risk—Look Before You Leap

Look before you leap, for as you sow, so shall you reap. Financial risk is often cheered when it leads to large rewards but decried when it ends in failure. In this chapter and the next we'll address some of the inconsistent thoughts, beliefs, or attitudes, especially as they relate to the behavioral decisions and attitude changes dealing with risk, particularly as it applies to retirement risk. We'll specifically look at one of the most deceptive and dangerous myths in the investment advisor's playbook; that stocks are safe in the long run. I will explain why this is so misleading. We'll also try to uncover some of the hidden traps that get in the way of good, solid decision making.

We are going to talk about **hype**, which I refer to sometimes as "look over here(s)." They are one-sided, overly enthusiastic explanations and promotions. We will talk about the **hope**, an all too often common theme, both in human nature and in financial planning. I once heard hope summarized as self-deception in pursuit of optimistic ends, and I think this is an accurate viewpoint. And lastly, we will talk about **theory fabrication**. This is the stretching of otherwise accurate assumptions into the overstated, overused and dangerous talk about the power of time to dissolve or minimize risk to the point of little or even no concern.

With a better appreciation of why we fail to assess risk properly, we'll be in a better position to self-correct. The idea is to build your confidence and expedite good risk decisions once you are ready to fine tune your investment plan, whether you decide to reallocate assets in a different way or not.

To start, we need to define what we mean by risk. To build your own insight, ask yourself what risk means to you, based on your own exposures to risks—financial or otherwise. A few proposed definitions of risk, that commonly surface, include: the unknown, the chance that something harmful may happen, uncertain outcomes that may cause loss, and uncertainty that arouses fear.

Let's discard the idea that risk is nothing but the unknown, because risk is more than the ordinary uncertainty that surrounds our lives. By referring to harm, loss, and fear, the next three suggestions reflect one common fundamental characteristic of risk: Somebody must care about the consequences if uncertainty is to be understood as risk. The consequences must matter to someone to mean anything.

The 'caring' or 'mattering' must be present for it to be risky. It includes the 'cost' or impact of uncertainty as well as its subjective nature, or rather how it will affect the life or lives of those who it will matter to. So for our purposes here, the definition we will use is: Risk is uncertainty that will impact one's life and/or lifestyle. There are two prongs to this definition; one- the uncertainty, and two- why it matters. Both are significant.

More important than the odds of losing, beyond the stress associated with volatility, there are the consequences of the loss to consider. That is where life is impacted by the risk; by the consequences. What will life be like if your finances don't work the way you 'hope' based on the amount of risk you take? If you look to your retirement objectives, you look at the amount of income you will need to live the life you intend to live as benchmarks for measuring risk; you'll deepen your appreciation for keeping your goals and objectives in line with the risk you ultimately decide to take.

When it comes to investing, we've been well trained, or more accurately stated, deceived to believe that stocks are safe when held for a long time. Most hard-working people, saving for retirement were and are being lulled into believing that mantra much too faithfully. When the market plunged in the fall of 2008, it even took the experts and financial advisors by surprise, as it always does. Their surprise always seems misplaced to me. They know the market goes down as well as up, and yet, they are surprised by the timing of a big drop, always, no matter when the drop is. One of those things that make you say, hmmm…

When you consider risk, retirement investing, and retirement financial planning from the 'income planning' perspective you see things differently, particularly risk. Even though income based planning and investing for retirement is on the rise, you'll be part of the fortunate few exposed to this approach; which is from this safety and reality vantage point. Right now, you may not perceive the difference or therefore the value of this but by the end of the book, I think you will. It is a different distinction and very real one!

A recently retired woman who became my client of mine in 2011 told me how she felt as the markets spiraled down in 2008. Her words were, "I felt risk turn from the abstract to a gut-wrenching nightmare." She said it reminded her of the time she decided to wait in line to go bungee jumping.

At home, before leaving, it all sounded adventurous; it was exciting and she looked forward to it. Once in line and getting ever closer to the jumping off platform, her heart began to race, she got cold sweats, and her stomach was doing gymnastics, sensing the real danger of the situation. She acknowledged that the risk was always present; the cord could break, it might wrap around her neck, she could faint, or something unexpected could happen. She said it was all abstract; unreal, until she got near the danger and the risk became real. The risk equaled a possible consequence; her life could be over! Ultimately, she correctly assumed the risk was very, very small and jumped, screaming all the way and loving it.

Sadly, experiencing the gut-wrenching reality of that 2008 loss was even more real to her and to all too many people that retired in 2008 and several years thereafter. Their earning years were finished, their earning time horizon was over and it coincided with losing half of their money. Not a good or happy place to be.

Like many Americans, this bungee jumping client experienced loss in all her assets at once, including her family's savings for their grandchildren's college education, the value of their home, household savings, and their retirement accounts. She described herself as a consistent, prudent, long-term saver and investor, and further stated she 'thought' and was told she was invested in a moderately conservative portfolio. She was told she had a good balance and was diversified. She expressed surprise that she had been lured into taking much more risk than she would have knowingly done. Once the storm cleared, she promised herself to return to a better risk balance, one that is truly diversified.

In the wake of 2008, risky investments have been a source of anxiety for many people. With the new norm being large swings and market volatility, this is even truer for those closer to retirement. Decisions made with equanimity when the market was on the way up now seem impossibly risky. Many retirees today are looking for a less dangerous, less risky answer.

Hype Is Real... and it is real attractive too.

But how do you find the right risk balance, the best asset allocation? The solution starts with an adjustment of flawed risk perceptions. It's helpful to see through the many distortions that are regularly pitched our way to champion investment products that inherently have higher risk than what we are told, and what we are sold. Promotion is always powerful and, when it is persistent or clever, it breeds familiarity and even trust. Repetition has a way of becoming our 'truth' just because we have always 'heard' it. In my practice, I frequently hear people say, "I don't believe in this investment, I don't believe in that strategy." Well, it is valuable to take note. Investing, and retirement income planning is not a religion. There is nothing to believe in. You should not be making financial decisions based on what you 'believe'. Do your homework and find the facts. Make decisions on that!

Campaigns that advocate risk have played a big role in fostering the public comfort with stock, bond and mutual fund ownership even though the hardworking 'investor' typically understands very little of the 'true' risk that is involved. To get a sense of the great influence these risk advocates have, I challenge you to look at the so-called educational content provided by investment industry sponsors, the financial media, and even government regulators in the financial realm. There is a ton of "stuff" out there, particularly on the Internet. The challenge is to glean anything in the way of real meaningful understanding from any of it.

What you will find are the things that we have all, always heard.

They are still saying the same old "stuff" that failed big-time in 2008. Buy stocks to ensure you achieve the return you need on your investments. Diversify, and hold your stocks for a long time more than 10 years, and preferably for 15 years or more. Market statistics and history are twisted to demonstrate that caution does not pay. The inference is as always, that you must take risk to make money.

Paul Samuelson, a Nobel laureate, wrote a 1994 article about the "Long-Term Case for Equities and How It Can Be Oversold" that is worth reading. Even the investor education provided by government agencies such as the Securities and Exchange Commission, which you might expect to be impartial, mostly presents a pitch that supports these old, over used, and oversold recommendations.

There are many online financial "wizards;" software programs and calculators that claim they will come up with a "personal" retirement portfolio tailored to your risk. I suggest you Google "asset allocation calculator" and try a few. If you do you are likely to find the same thing I did. Each calculator asks a few simple questions with slight variation, to set some narrow parameters: Age (or investment horizon, or years until retirement), and risk tolerance. Some have more whistles and bells, such as the amount of money desired and the amount of money available to invest. But all were simple and brief, meant as quick guides.

Most of the interactive calculators give the "appearance" of providing the opportunity to adjust risk to your personal preferences. They ask about your risk tolerance, and you can choose low, medium, or high, or in some cases you can opt for none. Typically, these calculators follow up with a question about flexibility in missing your objective with another choice; great, small, or nonexistent?

When I tried this on many calculators, I set my risk tolerance to zero. Regardless of the fact I stated that I wanted to take no risk, I kept getting a portfolio with 60 percent invested in stocks, if the time horizon exceeded 15 years. It was only when I shortened the time line to 10 years that the risk allocation fell, but only by a little, to 50 or 55 percent stocks. When I reduced this time horizon down to 3 to 5 years, I got a much smaller stock risk allocation, but it still came in at 25 percent. Even then it is assumed the rest of the money, the 75 percent remaining, should be in bonds. As if there is no risk with bonds. Remember 2008 disproved that clearly. Bonds lost value also. So, what might the real risk be with even 25 percent stocks and 75 percent bonds? We can only guess, or "hope." That is why it is called risk! Bonds represent a different type of risk. Bonds do not guarantee less risk.

In other words, the algorithms behind these wizards placed nearly all their weight on time horizon. Even zero risk tolerance translated into a portfolio leaning 60-40 stock-bond allocation. Time, if you are to believe the wizards, cures every possible problem. This is not true, and it is potentially, financially harmful for people in or near retirement! The earning years are near or behind you. The spending years are close at hand or have begun and that is a whole different rodeo. I do not need to remind anyone that we have a shorter time horizon in retirement. You might think I am talking about longevity here, and though longevity is a factor, what I am primarily talking here is your 'income' time horizon. When will you need the money? Do you want to make certain it is there when you need it?

The idea that time erases risk is so prevalent, and so wrong, that we will spend much of the next chapter talking about that. Risk, or more accurately, too much risk in retirement can be devastating. For now, let's summarize by saying that the argument for time diversification comes from a convoluted version of a more rigorously correct statement. But it is mathematically incorrect. Numbers are manipulated, and cleverly stated to make the argument that the chances of loss decline over time, but let's assume for a moment it was true. Even so this hardly means that the odds of loss or even large loss are zero, or negligible, just because the horizon is long. To evaluate risk, as we noted earlier, you need to know more than just the odds of losing. You also need to understand and appreciate the effects of losing; the damage if you will. That is the biggest price of risk. Neither these asset allocation calculators or software programs nor the type of planning typically done for retirees by most advisors does anything to address the magnitude of potential losses. They are also silent about investor goals, objectives and the resulting pain when these objectives are not met. Though the frequency of loss (odds) has the ability to smooth out (or average out) over long periods, the size of potential losses actually gets larger, not smaller, over time. The markets always go up, and go down but the longer your money is at risk the greater the chance you will incur a BIG loss. That is never mentioned.

The False Belief That Risk Will Shield you from Inflation

When researching available educational resources for retirees, I was not too surprised to find a video clip on the web site of the Financial Industry Regulatory Authority (FINRA), an independent industry self-regulatory organization. The clip depicted a young, good-looking couple (of course) preparing dinner together in a well-appointed kitchen, a scene very easy and comfortable for everyone to relate to. They were exchanging opinions about where they should be investing. Husband and wife portrayed as ordinary, prudent people and not greedy high rollers. Still, the wife informed her husband that it was too risky for them not to be in stocks. "TOO RISKY," **not be in stocks.** Let me understand; you must take risk to avoid risk. Hmmm?

The prudent, attractive young lady in the FINRA clip justified her 'scripted' opinion with another scripted statement, inferring that inflation would take too big of a toll if we don't take risk. As if risking loss is the best way to deal with inflation. Yikes. The only other option referred to was bank CDs. Explaining that, though the CDs might seem safe because they are insured (up to a maximum principal amount) they couldn't possibly keep pace with inflation. Therefore, the timid choice, the CD choice, means that protecting your money is actually the riskier choice. Unspoken message being; don't be timid because risk is safer. Hard to believe, but so many people fall for this, given no reason not to.

Is this a principle you've been trained to believe? I must say, I showed this to several people that I consider to be above average intelligence and asked them their opinion, whether they agreed or not. Three for three fell for it, and agreed with it. What!? The fact that this not so subtle promotion of risk was on an industry self-regulatory website, is at best duplicitous and self-serving. But when

I asked the three individuals queried, does this ring true when you think about 2000 and 2008 they all three agreed the principle put forth by FINRA was not what they experienced. Then when further told, in spite of the unparalleled growth in the market since 2009, adjusted for inflation, most people have not even maintained the spending power their money once had. Once they understood they were risking big losses and in many cases not even keeping up with inflation, they were quite surprised. They ended up confused but were at least questioning what is almost always presented and believed as the 'conventional wisdom'. This is a good start, one that could lead to change. This video was not an obscure footnote buried in some little looked at website. Furthermore, it was a common thread and narrative in most of the "educational" web sites we looked at.

It would be wonderful if stock market returns turn out to protect owners against inflation. There is the notion that businesses or companies (that you own stock in) can dodge inflation by raising prices. The truth, though, is less reassuring. Firms can't arbitrarily raise prices and maintain the same level of business. That is not how it works. And there is no real evidence whatsoever of a close relationship between stock returns and inflation. The best that can be said is that the data is not supported. There is almost no evidence at all that stocks can provide immediate protection against long-term inflation, and even some evidence to the contrary. The fact that inflation rates differ around the globe further muddies the picture, particularly in the new global economy.

Oddly, the seductive video on the FINRA website made no mention of other instruments that actually can provide inflation protection while protecting your money. It quite deceptively sets up a false either-or comparison between stock market risk and the low returns of the money market, or other short-term cash like investments, all very vulnerable to real losses through inflation. But the video, along with scores of other teaching tools on- and off-line, made no mentions of TIPS, I Bonds, annuities or other possible options.

It is a story, a pitch if you will, that is psychologically quite seductive and believable because it is so prevalent and frequently represented. But there are two important errors. One by commission and one by omission, that are worth paying attention to because they so distort the perception of the real risk associated with market volatility.

Target-Date Funds—The Deception

Many retirees find comfort in target-date funds, also known as 'retirement date' funds, based on the year you anticipate retiring. If you expect to retire in 2020, you may own a '2020 Fund' in your 401(k). These funds are designed to make investing simple by reducing their level of investment risk over time. Participants choose a date as close as possible to their planned retirement date. The funds start out in riskier investments, in search of higher returns. Gradually, as the target date approaches, they shift their holdings into theoretically at least, lower-risk assets. It is almost always a change in the allocation of assets, almost always more towards bond mutual funds than stock mutual funds as you age and get closer to retirement. Problem is in 2008, retirees and soon to retire people lost a lot of money with bonds and bond funds too. It is no longer true that bonds won't go down when stocks go down.

Because they are represented as simple with little thought necessary by the retiree/saver/investor, because of the innocuous name, 'target date funds', and by the nature of the fact that they are in our employer's 401(k) retirement plan, and many people take that path, there is a certain amount of safety assumed. Key word, 'assumed'. This is one reason so many people –unsuspecting, vulnerable people fall prey to the allure. They expect or believe these funds will provide balance, hence diversification, hence safety. The equation of (Stocks + Bonds) = Balance = Diversification = Protection IS INCORRECT and UNSUPPORTED BY THE FACTS.

Evidence of that fact became all too real to so many trusting workers, thinking they were doing the right thing when 2008 struck, the year that the S&P 500 (the index of the largest 500 U.S. public companies) fell 41 percent. That year most people lost 30 to 50% of their hard-earned 401(k) money. Research shows that the average target-date fund with a target date of 2010 lost between 24 percent and 41 percent. This happened within 2 short years of their supposed target date, or retirement date to make it real. What would it mean to you to lose that much of your money that close to retirement? Think seriously about that because contained within your answer will be the 'result' of risk that we spoke of earlier. The result of the loss is really the larger part, the more real part of risk. Yes, you lose assets, but the result or effect on your life is what is felt. It turns out that these target date funds were not a safe investment. There were no guarantees and insufficient protection. And unfortunate, as too many retirees found the name of the investment was cruel and deceptive; a case of half-truths and misdirection.

Many also learned other things that are disturbing. Once they really started digging, they found the funds' objectives and practices hard to ferret out, and there is considerable variation among different fund families. They realized that many of them used different ways to describe and measure risk, which makes it impossible to make much sense of. One thing in common among all those queried after the loss was that they were shocked at how these funds were explained using terms like "moderate" and "conservative." Do you consider it a conservative investment if you could possibly lose 40% or more within two years of retiring? One must ask at least, is this deception intentional?

One would think that something called a target date fund, masquerading as a good plan for retirement, would promise a specific amount, or at a minimum guaranteed range, at the target date. Instead, they appeared to be yet one more way for an investor to take on risk while they think they are deciding to avoid or at least minimize risk. If we can safely assume that 100% of these advisor/sales people cannot claim they do not know the truth, that makes it unconscionable.

The underlying message to emerge from all this hype has been inescapable: In the long run, the stock market can only go up. Its ascent is inexorable and predictable. Long-term stock returns are near certain while risks appear minimal, and only temporary. And the messaging has been effective: The familiar market propositions come across as bedrock fact. For the most part, the public views them as scientific truth, although this is hardly the case.

Was the 401(k) Designed to Benefit You?

It may surprise you, but all this 'market' confidence is rather new. Prevailing attitudes and behavior before the early 1980s were different. Fewer people owned stocks then, and the general popular attitude to buying stocks was wariness, not ebullience or complacency or what has recently become also known as 'blind faith'.

Our parents, and relatives of a generation ago—what I call the "pension generation"—typically avoided stocks. Today though, there is a much bolder, and I believe a more gullible attitude among the 401(k) generation. Have you ever wondered what happened? We might tend to think that our parents and grandparents were living with the outdated legacy of the Depression. But the bigger truth lies in the fact that most people today do not have a pension. The only real option we have been presented with is the 401(k). Along with that came no real or accurate unbiased education. The American public's embrace of stocks is not all related, or in many cases even... remotely related to the spread of sound knowledge. It's useful to consider how the transition evolved.

Let's look at a few of the key plot lines. Far from signaling the march of scientific progress, the taming of the investor perceptions traces back primarily to a gradual shift in pension fund arrangements since the 1970s and early 1980s. That's when a steady evolution began taking away defined benefit plans (pensions) and moving toward defined contributions plans (401(k)) and other plans like them. The fact that they were tax deferred was the big carrot that cemented the deal. They like us to believe, as the story goes, that this transition was, almost accidental, beginning in 1980. I don't believe it. Think about it for a minute. If you were a stock market professional, earning your living and/or family wealth from market related activities, would it not be a dream come true to have baby boomers put $16 Trillion dollars into 'your' stock market game and especially since, they know nothing about how to play? Just sayin'.

Over time, defined contribution plans, 401(k) type plans have come to eclipse traditional pension plans by a huge margin. An important upshot of this trend has been that the risk, as well as the task, of how to fund retirement has moved from employer to you, the employee. Who did that benefit, you? It's hard to overemphasize the importance of this transformation to the way Americans invest today, or more accurately, financially prepare for the retirement years.

The great pension makeover set a retail stock market investment boom in motion. It pulled billions of dollars of hard working Americans into the stock market via 401(k)s and mutual fund investing. To get an idea of how explosive the expansion has been, consider that in 1984 there were 459 equity mutual funds in the United States. By 2008, there were 4,830—and they held about $3.75 trillion.

It was sold to us gradually. Most people don't realize, or remember that 401(k) plans were originally intended (sold) as a supplement to defined benefit pensions. It made some sense for their owners then to take higher risk in search of higher investment returns, because the basics—the guaranteed income retirees need; was largely assured via pension and Social Security. If you recall how we distinguished needs, or essentials, from wants, or extras earlier in the book, then it's easy to see that the 401(k)s started out as vehicles to fund the aspirational goals, the extras. For in the beginning of the transition, workers and employees typically had traditional pensions and Social Security to cover basic needs.

Fast forward to today, and we find 401(k)s are no longer supplements to pension plans. They must provide for the basic needs as well as the extras. Quite different! Thus, the amount of risk a 401(k) investor should be taking must be considered under current realities. Key here –"should be taking." What the 401(k) was originally intended to provide, the extras, has morphed without us realizing it. But, the risk remains the same or even higher, at a time when we need to count on our retirement money to provide future needs, not just the extras.

With the government given 'incentive' of tax deferral, we took the bait! Other retirement savings plans have also grown in scale and availability—including plans for the self-employed, plans for nonprofit and government employees, and more. They are not restricted to equity investments, but the message from the retirement planning world has emphasized the stocks and stock mutual funds as the core of a "sensible" long-term investing strategy, no matter what type of tax deferred (qualified) plan you have.

Yes, the word is out. In the 1970s, stock ownership (including mutual funds) was limited to about one in four or five American households. By 2008, nearly half of American households owned stock. Equity ownership peaked at about 53 percent just before the market decline of 2001, but in light of the recent market growth, the numbers are on the increase again. We seem to forget so quickly. The problem is that this message, that stocks and stock mutual funds are the core of a "sensible" long-term investing strategy; comes with all the distortions we've been discussing. Unfortunately, unbiased, and factual information, free of selective omission, is not easy to come by, for the reasons I have stated above.

The Mirage of a Long Bull Market

If stocks had remained in the doldrums or in decline, the surge in their popularity may never have happened. In tandem with the redrawing of the retirement pension map though, the U.S. stock market took off. In 1983, the S&P index rose at a steady pace that continued more or less without a hitch until a sudden dramatic collapse that took people by surprise. That was in 1987, and it was the first market collapse I experienced as a financial professional. The breakdown of October 1987 was quickly ironed out, partly through actions of the Federal Reserve. The S&P returned to its pre-crash level in less than a year. For the next 12 years, the market resumed its upward climb, taking only a few short breathers here and there until 2000.

In retrospect, the quick restoration of stock market value that followed the 1987 decline in part encouraged people to ignore market volatility as a message about risk. To the contrary, an almost automatic pattern of (attempts at) opportunistic "buying on the dips" developed. The common view at that time held that the slumps would be short-lived, and so it appeared to be so. The run-up of stock prices in the 1980s and especially the 1990s promoted a self-reinforcing faith in the 'market' as the road to sure riches. The creation of the 401(k) and IRA investment options provided a way for the 'average' person to reap the rewards, or so it seemed. Many individuals who might not otherwise have found the means to buy stocks or stock mutual funds were able to do so easily, by using the savings in their retirement accounts, which often included matching contributions from employers. By the way, have you noticed, the employer match has steadily become a shrinking carrot and for many has disappeared?

It's hard to underestimate the persuasive power of the long bull market. Earlier generations had been warned off stocks following the collapses that took place after the Roaring Twenties Depression and after the Go-Go Sixties market decline of the 1970s. The late-20th century bull market ran long and strong enough to convince a massive following, mainly Baby Boomers, of its enduring profitability. An entire cohort of Baby Boomers was educated at its knees. Even if the ascent got interrupted from time to time, it seemed as though it would not end. Unfortunately, it may also be the 'thing' that brings Baby Boomers... to their knees. To say that the market's nearly steady upward run has masked the true inherent risk is an understatement.

The Internet Fuels the Fire

The growing appetite for stock ownership found further encouragement in another new trend—one that traced its early origins back to 1979—the buying and selling of securities online by consumers, without ever talking to a broker. The rise of personal computing and the Internet brought well known change to consumer stock trading. The investment industry took advantage of new cyber opportunities, offering a widening array of trading, portfolio management, and research tools online. A retail financial supermarket, an idea dreamed up more than 30 years ago, became a thriving reality. To this chorus of champions, the media also lent its voice, through a few dedicated financial cable networks, cheerleading financial web sites, TV talking heads, pseudo financial gurus and more. Expansionary growth cycled faster and bigger in the decade of the 1990s, eventually fueling a speculative investment trend that culminated in the dot-com bubble bursting in 2000. This 'caution to the wind' attitude by investors and financial advisors eventually imploded, bringing with it a recession and considerable pain. The pain is always felt more by retirees and the soon to retire because they no longer have the same time to get their money back as they once did.

Lessons were learned. By defining it as the 'dotcom' bust, they worked hard to keep the principal cautionary message narrow. By and large, the inherent riskiness of stocks outside the technology sector escaped widespread and fundamental scrutiny. That is what I call a 'look over here'. Look over here where rapid stock churning, speculation and day trading may not be good for your future, but... don't look over there where you will find so many others that lost a ton of money too, even though you were not day trading or churning. The numbers bear this out. Despite the market's decline in 2001 and 2002, individual investors continued until the end of 2003 to express great confidence that it would rebound within the coming year. The confidence index then, according to the data collected by the Yale School of Management, stood at a remarkable 95.62 percent. Confidence levels fell in 2005 and 2006, but now are below the 80 percent mark.

Thanks to the ever-skillful present proselytizing and the memory of the market's long bull run, people continued to underrate risk. Against the evidence and against the science, the flawed conventional theories endured. It would take one more market collapse in the space of just a few years and a bone-cracking one at that to create some doubt, some concern and to begin a reassessment by many. Something was not right, was the underlying theme. Memories are short and humans are naturally optimistic. Even after 2000 and 2008, despite a flood of regret and re-evaluation, and a newfound interest in understanding risk, very little has changed. Even after seeing the devastation done to the lives of their co-workers, family and friends that retired in and around 2008, most people retiring within the next 5 years still have the majority of their money at risk. Do you?

Chapter 4
Takeaways

- Somebody must care about the consequences if uncertainty is to be understood as risk. The consequences must matter to someone to mean anything. Ask yourself, what are the consequences if my retirement plan fails? In other words, what does your life look like if you run out of 'enough' money to live on?
- The Wall Street answer for down markets is to just hold on, it will come back. For retirees, this is 'theory fabrication'. When you need money to live on you do not have a choice to 'hold on,' to wait, for the market to come back.
- Many risk type advisors would have you believe, all you need to do is take risk. The risk will (miraculously) always make you money and that growth will be a solution for future inflation. NOT!
- Retirees knew what they were going to live on when they had a pension. Most of us must figure that out. The 401(k) did not help us. It helped Wall Street and the income taxing authorities, the federal and state governments.
- A lot of people 'believing' the same things do not make them true. Look for the proof. Look for the truth and believe that.

*"Most of the problems in life are because of two reasons:
We act without thinking or we keep thinking without acting."*

Unknown

Chapter 5

Hope, Human Nature and Retirement

Our optimistic, human brains typically do not operate on the laws of probability, though it is a fact that that is exactly what rules the universe; probability. The largely believed credo, 'stocks are the best bet for the long haul' is due to a large degree to outside influence but also (we) have some responsibility for believing something that has little basis in reality. We have been willing collaborators in the deception. Emotional biases effect our perceptions, coaxing us to take the bait at nearly every turn, like the mouse that just cannot resist taking the cheese from the trap, even though he can see what happened to his 'mouse' friend. Humans are simply not wired well for judging risk.

Behavioral economists have amply demonstrated these cognitive failings in recent years and, as we discuss a few of them, you are likely to recognize them immediately, even if you've never heard of them before. In fact, one of the early and most recognized pioneers in the field, the late psychologist Amos Tversky, once modestly demurred that all he had to do was to employ scientific methods to examine behaviors that were well known to advertisers and used-car salesmen. Behavioral economists have done us a service by bringing the subject to the forefront, by encouraging us all to recognize the flaw in our ability to make decisions under uncertainty. Of course, recognizing it is one thing; heeding the warning, and tempering our penchant for risk is another.

As we're learning from psychology and neuroscience research, the human mind draws on two disparate ways of knowing. There is the part of us that intuits and the part that reasons. The two operating systems don't always work in concert. The intuitive brain is ruled by habit and emotion—and it tends to resist change. It regularly uses shortcuts to arrive at quick conclusions. When it's perceptions differ from the conclusions of the rational brain, it is the emotional side that prevails, more often than not. We are all literally of two minds, and our 'feelings', not our rational mind usually wins. So, when we see everyone else doing what they do with their hard-earned money, mainly taking risk, we say to ourselves, "Hey, it is what everyone is doing" and it makes us (feel) like we should do it too.

Unfounded Confidence

This duality is relevant to the way we tend to judge risk, intuitively, rather than via technical or rational measurements. Like the story earlier about the bungee jumping client, we tend to notice risk primarily when it stirs our emotions, until then it is not very tangible. Add to that when things are going well, investors typically exhibit overconfidence about their prospects. The undue confidence in their own abilities and/or their belief that their advisors are better educated 'guessers' leads them to underplay, or ignore the risks that they are taking. By the way, their advisors are typically better educated guessers, when it comes to buying decisions, but they are still guessing. Speaking of guessing, in the 80's *The Wall Street Journal* ran an article and experiment for years that was based on a hypothetical portfolio created by monkeys throwing darts at the stock page of the WSJ. Eventually, they had to stop because they were losing Wall Street advertisers because the monkeys won 49% of the time.

Excessive optimism helps explain the popularity of the stocks-for-the-long-run doctrine. The pseudo-factual statement that stocks always succeed in the long run provides an overconfident investor with more grist for the optimistic mill. To understand how easily investors, slide into overconfident patterns, it's worth knowing how common overconfident behavior is in general. Research has shown, for example, that people tend to rank themselves above average on just about all-favorable traits. Over-confidence extends beyond investment skill to driving ability, a sense of humor, and even expected longevity. In one often cited example, when American students were asked to rate their own driving safety more than three-fourths believed that were in the top third of the group. Seventy-five percent cannot be in the top one third! Not possible, right? Like these students, investors, even the soon-to-retire investors tend to think, if or better yet, when there is another big drop before they retire somehow, they will not be hurt as much as most people.

Overconfidence may get cultural reinforcement too. An international comparison of the math achievement of young pupils around the world placed U.S. students below the 10 ranked near the top, though the students were certain they were in the top ten percent. Overconfidence of Americans does not come as a surprise. After all we have been taught that we are exceptional, right? Common as it is, overconfidence is not universal. There is evidence, for example, that women are typically less confident and more risk averse, in their investment behavior than men. This difference probably holds in other realms as well, at least one study, for instance, has shown that women underestimate their own intelligence scores whereas men consistently overestimate theirs. Since I am a male, I hate to state this but, hey, it is true. Haha! But this is also changing for women as they embrace their confidence more frequently in the name of equality, which sometimes equates to being more like a man. This is not always a good thing, or maybe never a good thing. I dunno; that is a different book.

When thinking of risk, it's worth emphasizing that confidence or courage when taking risk differs from optimistic overconfidence. Psychologist Daniel Kahneman, winner of the 2002 Nobel Prize in Economics has made clear this central distinction. Speaking with the editors of Forbes.com in 2002, Kahneman explained: "Courage is willingness to take the risk once you know the odds. Optimistic overconfidence means you are taking the risk because you don't know the odds. It's a big difference."

Optimism can be a great motivator. It helps especially when it comes to implementing plans. But, although optimism is a good thing, it's not always appropriate. You would not want your retirement professional wearing rose-colored glasses. You want him to see things clearly and realistically and communicate them as such, without bias. Hard to do when your income is associated with the rose-colored glasses (risk).

The Illusion of Control

Overconfident or not, almost everyone can recognize some aspects of themselves in a cluster of related behaviors. These habits are so common that they don't stand out, yet they subtly subvert our ability to assess risk. By learning to spot them in action, we can start to break their hold.

First, there is the confidence that flows from a sense of control—whether real or imagined. Abundant evidence suggests that people do feel more secure when they believe they are in control—even when they plainly are not. There are travelers, for example, who fear flying, although they're quite comfortable behind the wheel of a car. Statistically, they have it backwards—the odds of serious mishap on the highway greatly outweigh the risks of air travel. But on the road, they occupy the driver's seat, and that seems to make all the psychological difference. The common global phenomenon of driver overconfidence may similarly stem from the illusion of control.

In another example of the illusion of control and its consequences, participants in a coin-tossing experiment bet more money when given the chance to call heads or tails before the coin was tossed than *after*. Apparently, calling the coin after it had been tossed exposed the entirely speculative nature of the game, while choosing the 'call in advance' imparted an illusion of influence over the result, when there is none. Calling before or after the toss does not change the chance of winning.

Researchers report similar patterns among buyers of lottery tickets. Buyers strongly prefer to choose the number they're betting, rather than passively accepting a computer-generated number. Active involvement gives them a sense of empowerment against the odds—even though the control is illusory. Don't believe it? Just go to a 7-11 the day before the next Super Lotto and stand around as people buy their tickets.

The problem is that illusions of control bring a false sense of mastery over risk. This has the effect of making risk even riskier. The illusion of information can also feel equally aggrandizing. The fault here may lie deep in the human brain. More than we realize, we rely on context for most of our perceptions—of size, for example, or loudness, or distance. If you are seated in a dark room, looking at a bright object with no clues about how close or far away that object actually is, it's impossible to make a good judgment about its size. Lacking the necessary information, though, our minds will jump to conclusions and deliver a clear impression–one that appears incontrovertibly true. In the absence of necessary information, the brain seems to reflexively fill in the gaps with its own interpretation.

The trouble is that we can't distinguish between factual evidence and manufactured shortcuts to interpretation. Turn the lights back on, and you may be amazed that the bright object is far smaller and farther away (or larger and closer) than you had imagined. If you were to gather the outcomes of your financial bets (or decisions), with 20/20 hindsight you would likely see how skewed your assumptions were there too, all too often.

Illusions of information and control can lead to magical thinking. The gamblers who favored coin-tosses they could call in advance are a prime example. So, too, are investors who were gulled into fraudulent Ponzi schemes with unrealistic expectations. The same can be said about the many other investors who planned to save little but reap bounteously, based on great timing and supersized returns. For them, it will likely be a very rough landing as they come to the end of the run way and pull up to the Retirement Tower.

Some psychologists have theorized that magical or wishful thinking is a protective cloak that people slip into when confronting complex matters that seem beyond their comprehension. Please take a moment here and ask yourself, 'what is my real comprehension of what is happening with my money? What could happen with my money? Then factor in the exponent of being near retirement. Too often, the uncontrollable and the unknowable generate so much frustration, helplessness, and even anger that many people invoke fantasy as a way to limit and deal with the confusion. Either way, whether using a reflexive interpretation or protective distraction, wishful thinking frequently, and in a big way undermines rational decision-making in uncertain situations.

Perspective

Also, we are vulnerable to the way things are presented to us. Our susceptibility to framing makes us easy to manipulate and is another wellspring for overconfidence, illusory knowledge, and flawed estimation of risk.

As Madison Avenue, oh... and Wall Street has long understood, framing and innuendo have great unconscious power to shape our attitudes and actions. It's well known that vendors can fool consumers with their choice of words. Sort of like when they tell you at Ralph's grocery store every time you check out, how much money you saved. "Thanks for shopping at Ralphs. You saved $27.82 today." Every time the cashier says that to me, I ask, "Where is it?" Just by the nature of the fact I did not pay $27.82 'more' for the groceries DOES NOT MEAN I 'SAVED' ANYTHING. Really, who do they think they are fooling? A lot of people, not just me. I accept the reality that I spent $96.50, I DID NOT SAVE anything! Their marketing research shows many people are fooled by that little twist of reality, causing them to 'think' shopping at Ralph's is cheaper, a deal if you will. People are more likely to buy a big screen TV, a car or other big ticket purchases when they are framed as an 'investment'. Come on, really? Has anyone ever earned money reselling a car or TV? The very same principle applies when people 'believe' they haven't lost until they sell. Nonsense! The money is G O N E.

In a similar vein, individuals display illogical preferences depending on whether there is a subpar option available to them or not. In one well-known study, people were offered either a set amount of cash or a luxury Cross-pen of equal value. Only a third of them chose the pen. But if their available choices were widened to include the Cross pen, the same set amount of cash, and an inferior pen as well, far more people chose the Cross pen. When comparisons are offered, things can be made to look suddenly good. Yes, it is funny... but true. True when it comes to saving and investment decisions too.

How you frame something, or how perspective is used comes into play in surprising ways. Another well-known inconsistency that almost all of us display is to apply a different yardstick depending on whether we are an outsider or an insider. If you've read through these various scenarios and illustrations of illogical behavior but dismissed them as characterizing "other people" and not you, maybe it's time to think again. Difficult as it may be, try rereading them in the first person singular, and listen for resonance.

Framing exerts potent influence on the perception of risk, especially when it comes to weighing losses and gains. People hate to lose even more than they like to win. They act differently, depending on whether they are presented with the prospect of a sure gain and the possibility of an equal loss. People overwhelmingly avoid risk and stick with the sure gain.

Interestingly, though, this behavior reverses when the choice is between a certain loss and a possible gain. To avoid the sure loss, most people now become willing to take risks they would otherwise shun. Thus, in order to avoid losing $100 for sure, they become irrationally willing to risk losing much more than $100—in exchange for the (small) chance they may end up losing nothing. One of those things that make you say, "Hmmm."

Losses can be insidious, in other words, because they summon emotions rather than reason in their wake. Loss can, and regularly does, induce people to throw good money after bad in hopes of recovering what they once had. If, however, the same risky investment is framed outside the individual's prior loss, chances are that he or she will reconsider and act more rationally. This reminds me of trip to Las Vegas with a friend. On the airplane he said, "I enjoy gambling but I only brought $500 to play (gamble) with. I just look at it as part of my entertainment." Later that night, sitting at a blackjack table, after losing his $500, he did not hesitate to loss another $1,000 trying to get back the $500 he lost. The next day, when the emotion of having lost the $500 was one night removed, he quipped, "It was not very smart of me to lose another $1,000 trying to get back the $500 I lost."

We need to recognize the odd nexus between losses and a willingness to take more risk. An example is a client I have that is still angry with her ex-husband for taking too much risk in their pre-2007 portfolio and losing so much money. She has realized that her raw feelings have made her susceptible to large swings in the way she regards risk—dismissively on some days and with great concern on others. She no longer 'believes' (there is that believing again) that she should ever have any money 'in the market'. Firstly, this is an emotionally skewed decision, not fact based. Nevertheless, it led her to consider an early stage investment in a company where she knows the principal. She originally 'felt' (emotion again) secure in the high returns the owner talked about. She thought her inside knowledge would ensure success. After talking through it with us, she was able to at least acknowledge that the insider 'feeling' really did nothing to lessen the risk. Now she's not so sure if she will invest in the startup. The point being, it 'might' be great it 'might, not'. Recognize the reality and de-emphasize the 'feeling' you get from knowing the owner and then decide.

There is another, often overlooked and maybe more important point in this story. It is the blame game. Most people blamed their advisors, the market, luck and other things when they lost money in 2008. But the fact is that only they were the one in control of deciding the amount of risk they would take. Ultimately, if one losses money, it is because (they) decided to take the risk. Whether they understood the risk or not, may be a question, but never the less, they made the decision. No one is forced to take more risk than they want to. That said, so very many otherwise very intelligent people, decide to risk their financial future following the crowd, in a lackadaisical way, and with little misunderstanding. I do not pretend to know how much risk is right for you. I do not know you or your situation. But, I do know you should not be risking the majority of your retirement nest egg without understanding the facts.

Losing money is inherent, it goes hand in hand with investing in unsure investments, and so does earning money. Problem is we don't know when we will earn or when we will lose. There is no way to time the earning of money to when we will need it for income. It is okay, and in some cases a good idea to take risk, but for retirees or soon to retire individuals, they should not be taking more risk than their lifestyle can afford. Retirees and the soon to retire need to coordinate risk with when you will need to spend the money.

Another illusion of control is doing nothing. Like a client that came in because she inherited $180,000. She does not want to lose anything so she becomes paralyzed and does nothing. She feels that doing nothing is somehow control; a kind of status quo confidence that she realizes is foolish but can't seem to shake. What she is doing is locking in the very real loss to inflation. One must realize that deciding to 'do nothing' is... ah, a decision. In her case a decision to lose 3% a year, give or take, of her spending power. This really adds up. Well, technically, it really takes away!

It's useful to reflect on your own perceptions about risk. Do you recognize yourself in any of the behavioral patterns? Have hype, the overly optimistic allure of hope, and the status quo of doing nothing colored your reflexive assumptions about investment risk?

Probability Blindness

As we've noted, the popular perception of risk as 'benign in the long run' also stems from another key cognitive shortcoming, known as probability blindness. Thanks to probability blindness, the notion that risk fades with time remains stubbornly sticky. And yet, most of us know in our bones that uncertainty does not fade over time. The weather is a good example. Which do you trust more, the 10-day prediction or tomorrow morning's report?

Dueling Intuitions

Think about this: A person's lifetime risk of cancer is plainly greater than the risk of getting cancer before the age of 40. So, too, the risk that there will be a fatal airline crash over, say, the Andes, is higher over a 10-year period than in any single year. With increased exposure comes mounting risk.

Similarly, if you take a shortcut as you walk home each day, cutting across a busy highway on your way, your risk of being hurt on any single crossing may not make you nervous but over the course of the year, crossing that busy highway 200 plus times, as the uncertainty grows, the odds of mishap increase. If you are a skilled parachutist who jumps, for fun, out of an airplane once a month, your risk of having an accident is going to be greater over the coming year than on any one jump. Over the long haul, the more you are exposed to danger, the more likely it is to catch up with you. The odds don't exactly add, but they do accumulate.

Yet, overriding this instinctive understanding, the prevailing investment dogma told us just the reverse. The creed that stocks grow steadily safer over time, buy and hold has managed to trump our common sense by appealing to a different set of self-serving precepts.

Chief among these is a flawed surmise that, with the passage of time, downward fluctuations are balanced out by compensatory upward swings. Many people believe that each step backward will be offset by more than one step forward. The assumption is that you will always, 'have more' later. That is true… until it's not! If the 'not' happens to coincide with retirement like it did for too many in 2008, the damage is done and mostly unable to be repaired. Your retirement life will now need to be recast, redefined based on significantly less assets.

Though it is rarely talked about and readily rationalized away in the 'selling' process, it must be made clear, that the opposite of the above is also just as true. With the passage of time upward swings are and historically always balanced out by the downward fluctuations too! Yes, yes I know, over time, historically markets have always 'come back' and gone higher. So what!!! Even assuming this will always be true; the thing overlooked and never asked is, "Will it come back in time for me, for my purpose? Will it come back when I need the money?"

Today's faith in stocks as a safe long-term investment owes much of its traction to the best-selling book, *Stocks for the Long Run*, by Wharton professor Jeremy Siegel, which first appeared in 1994. Siegel collected copious data reaching back to 1802 and concluded that over long periods (possibly 17 years or more), stocks had beaten nominal government bonds hands down. Far more than bonds, he said, stocks possessed the ability to preserve purchasing power over the long run and the short-run volatility of stocks calmed down, over the long run, providing investors with a secure investment return.

As we've seen, Siegel's thesis has taken root, so much so that it has become a near-foundational belief. As we found out when playing with automated allocation wizards online, we are hard pressed to find an educational website where the theory, the myth if you will, that investing in a 'balanced' portfolio of stocks and bonds will always work out over the long haul. Part of the argument's allure is its optimism. We've already observed how emotion, promotion, and cognitive error can help pave the way for flawed perception. And, there is no question that Siegel's contentions about safety lost much of their nuance as they were recast into sound bites and slogans. Stocks were regularly presented as if they were as riskless over the long run as default-free government bonds. What a deal.

One of Siegel's followers went to absurd extremes. In 1999, James K. Glassman and Kevin A. Hassett published the now infamously titled *Dow 36,000*.5 (In 1999, the Dow Jones Industrial Average was fluctuating between 10,000 and 11,000). Glassman and Hassett claimed that stocks were not very risky, and were therefore mispriced by people who believed they were. This widespread error presented a fabulous opportunity in their view. Once the rest of the market came to its senses and realized the mistake, the Dow would reach 36,000.

But Siegel's case has a serious core. Although we can dismiss some of its most extravagant distortions we can't just leave it at that. We will also have to address the basic intuition that instills so much reflexive trust in its adherents; the presumption is that the up-and-down fluctuations of the market cancel out during any individual's personal investment horizon. Seen in this light, short run riskiness melts into long-run safety. This is nothing more true than if you cross that dangerous highway more times it becomes less risky. It's urgent to resolve the contradiction. The safety of your investment goals, the security of your retirement depends on it.

The Perils of Probability

The stocks-for-the-long-run vision is based on some rigorously demonstrable truths about prospective returns and some highly misleading conclusions about risk. That's why we have characterized it as theory fabrication. The case relies heavily on the expectation that shortfalls will be overwhelmed by upward growth over time. Despite the accessibility of this intuition, it creates the false impression that a cycle of loss-offsetting gains is something anyone can capture simply by being patient. Not to mention the very big fact that fees, costs, charges and inflation must be factored into any real conclusion. Oh and by the way, as a retiree, past the earning years, patience is not always an option. There are bills to pay and we must eat.

But here's the deal. Stock returns are random. They resist close prediction. Even if long-run stock returns keep coming back to their own historical trend line, stock prices still move randomly. Proponents of stocks for the long run generally support this idea of so-called mean reversion, but even in this rendition, random noise buffets the annual returns in unexpected ways. No one knows exactly what the path of stock returns will look alike. There could be large swings or small, very long runs or extremely short ones. The path could include many above-or below average years in a row. Mean reversion, if it happens at all, could be accomplished quickly or extremely slowly. It is inattention to the role of randomness that lets us unthinkingly have the two dueling intuitions simultaneously. When it comes to chance and luck, most of us wear dark blinders.

Riddles of Randomness

A common device used to push the superiority of risk in the long run is to chart historical U.S. stock returns over very long terms. Lengthy tables like these are used to show that over very long holding periods (of 60 to 100 years), the average inflation-adjusted return on stocks is quite steady, hovering around 6.5 percent.

Many people take assurance from these numbers. But the reality is that these super long periods of time only hold advantage for institutions and the super wealthy that have generational money, or money they do not need. The time horizon for the average retiree has no relation to 60 to 100 years. But they still frequently buy into the irrelevant principle of buy and hold without serious consideration about how it does not fit their own circumstances.

Still, the promise of a continuous, steady return exerts a kind of magical charm. There is something we refer to as probability blindness. Stock prices move randomly—and these views profoundly miss that central point. The conventional faith in stocks for the long run shows how resistant we are to grasping the way randomness rules our lives. The issue is larger than ignorance, because experts or so called experts too, the ones with your retirement money, they too fall prey to confusion, optimism and unfortunately selfish motivation. As the scientist Stephen Jay Gould has put it, in his memorable essay about streaks in baseball... and in life, "If we understood Lady Luck better, Las Vegas might still be a road stop in the desert."

Instead of accepting fact and reality, we seem to be motivated much more by the stories that 'infer' predictable patterns to our investment returns. And the backstory is that losses are destined to be offset by larger gains, so just hang in there. An irrational rationale, if you will. This hard to understand thinking has most investors and money managers highlighting the bull market years, bragging about returns of 10%, 12% and higher. Hey get your money invested! With their reality blinders on they ignore the fact that, adjusted for inflation, the money most investors have 'in the market' today is not even worth what it was in 2000. Depending on fees, they may well be at a loss. Yes, a loss after 16 years of roller coaster risk and willingness to bear 50% losses. Some investors mistakenly 'think' they have made money when they have not, once adjusted for inflation and fees. They have short memories and, oh... they have been adding money to their retirement account over these years too. That is often at a minimum, part of the reason the account has gone up.

Our failure to comprehend probability has been the subject of several recent books, all studded with entertaining but disconcerting stories about how reliably we misunderstand the role of chance. Is there anyone that doubts the role of randomness in the stock market today, up 200 points one day and down the 300 the next? Really? Can the economy, the global financial world change that fast, and then back again the next day? In an interesting and applicable illustration, researchers recorded the sequence of one hundred actual coin tosses, and then inserted these results into a short list of made-up heads-and-tails sequences. They asked participants to find the one real sequence. Few succeeded since we commonly expected the results to show balance. The odds, after all, over the long haul (sound familiar?) are 50-50. But the truly random runs included long, imbalanced strings of successive heads or tails.

Look at streaks in baseball, basketball and "hot hands" in cards; these examples provide vivid examples of the same tendency. Hot hands in cards along with hitting streaks in baseball, and hot streaks in basketball are widely accepted as true and well-documented phenomena. As Stephen Jay Gould colorfully wrote, "You get that touch, build confidence; all nervousness fades, you find your rhythm; swish, swish, swish. Or you miss a few, get rattled, endure the booing, experience despair; hands start shaking and you realize that you should have stayed in bed."

The central conviction behind this belief is the premise that in normal play, scores and misses appear in virtually balanced succession. Long, uninterrupted runs appear to defy the odds—and are therefore best explained as personal acts of triumph, by athletes and fans alike. Hot hands don't really exist, any more than streaks and slumps do in baseball, the stock market, or in life. Psychologist Amos Tversky, together with Thomas Gilovich and Robert Vallone, studied the entire play of the Philadelphia 76ers and discovered that the odds of a player's scoring a second basket did not rise after a successful basket. In addition, the number of successful baskets by any player, whether runs or streaks were indistinguishable from the prediction of a random, coin-tossing model, where the odds of a score were the same for every shot. Of course, better players had better sequences—their overall odds of shooting a basket were better—but not beyond what could be predicted by the random probability model, in light of their overall past performance.

There are clear parallels with stock investing. Like sports, in the financial world to be the best is the goal, with money managers vying for that coveted top position each year. Someone must be this year's hero. But next year it is someone else. It is random. It would be as wrong to expect a smooth and predictable performance from stocks as it is from basketball players. In both instances, it is our probability blindness that dims our understanding. That blindness leads us to ascribe meaning where none exists. We interpret random sequences as hot hands; stock losses are understood as harbingers of future gains; hey today we lost, tomorrow we win.

Why we insist on finding our answers in stories instead of acknowledging the role of chance is not well understood. Gould has speculated that we may be seeking comfort, or struggling to keep confusion at bay. Some experts suggest that gains in our accounts, like streaks, hot hands, or winning bets are often more memorable than losses, and therefore cloud our judgment. Because we remember them more clearly than losses, we often believe they occur more often than they actually do. As humans, we just like a good, winning story more than a sad or bad ending. When the story has a good ending though, we ignore the role of luck and stress skill, good judgment and intentions instead. Tales about heroic athletes, and iconic financial figures and their specific achievements of all kinds win the day.

In these innate tendencies, our very nature may explain why we allow a faith in the long run to dominate 'safety' of truly risky investments. The concrete story prevails. It is, after all, about gains to be gained with supposed skill and then counted, savored, then consumed. Pitted against the more abstract and diffuse calculus of uncertainty, there is no contest, we love a winner! Better yet we like to be a winner. If we are to be a winner, we have been taught, we have to 'go for it!' Note: In the retirement game, it is not he who has the most money at retirement, it is the he that has the best plan for making it last!

No One Is Getting Out of Here Alive

By now it should be clear that the long run is an impossible standard to apply. Even more so when the 'long run' is no longer long. Ha! Not to get morbid.   I am not only referring to our mortality. Our time horizon in retirement is not only defined by our longevity. It can more often, and more importunately refer to the time between the day we retire and the day we need some of our retirement money. Is this a long haul or long time for you, or a short time? For some it might be right away and for others it might be 10 years. Every situation is different. But it should be easy to understand that even a 10-year time horizon is no 'long haul'!

If you are building a dynasty for the ages and have boundless resources, then stocks for the long run might be the best possible game plan. Losses should not faze you then. You'll never need to withdraw the money, and you'll have the resources to withstand all bear markets and if 'long haul' history repeats itself your heirs will thank you.

But for the rest of us, an extremely 'long-run standard' does not suit our finite assets or our mortal lives. As John Maynard Keynes said, "The market can stay irrational longer than you can stay solvent." As we've seen, target-date funds or other age-based strategies don't solve the problem because they may be locking in losses at just the moment when they are switching from stocks to bonds. To be clear, they switch from more stocks to more bonds as you age. It is age based decision, or action. The switch takes place no matter what the market is doing. So, people with a 2010 target date fund had 2008 losses locked in when their stocks were sold to buy bonds. Not good.

Markets rise and markets fall, but it is folly to assume that they'll hit their best averages in perfect rhythm with your retirement date and/or your specific timing and need for income. Instead of closing your eyes, crossing your fingers and placing your faith in the potential and timing of an indefinite long run, a more dependable decision for retirement is to focus on your specific needs, get educated so you better understand the financial realities of retirement and don't follow the herd.

When one says, "I usually have good intuition," they are stating that they 'think' or (intuit) their feelings are usually correct. Humans are of two minds. The intuitive brain is ruled by habit and emotion—and it tends to resist change. It regularly uses shortcuts to arrive at quick conclusions. When differing from the rational brain, it is the emotional side that usually prevails. So, when we see everyone else doing what they do with their hard-earned money, mainly taking risk, we say to ourselves, "Hey, it is what everyone is doing" and it makes us (feel) like we should do it too. You only get one shot at putting a plan in place to provide the income you will need to live on for the rest of your life.

Chapter 5
Takeaways

- Humans also tend to judge themselves more rational than they are and have a natural tendency towards optimism. Investors, even the soon to retire investors tend to think, if (when) there is another big drop they will not be hurt as much as most people.
- Confidence when taking risk differs from optimistic overconfidence. Confidence is the willingness to take the risk once you know the odds. Optimistic overconfidence is taking risk without 'truly' understanding the odds, often with an attitude of, "Hey, it will all workout." It is valuable to really 'get' the difference.
- It's useful to reflect on your own perceptions about risk. Do you recognize yourself in any of the behavioral patterns? Have hype, the overly optimistic allure of hope, and the status quo of doing nothing colored your reflexive assumptions about investment risk?
- For 55 and uppers with a decent nest egg, having a solid plan to make your money last as long as you do is as, or even more important than the size of the nest egg.
- The time horizon for risk in retirement is defined by when we will need the money, not how long we will live. You may live another 25 or 30 years but need some of your money to live on in 5 or 10.
- "The market can stay irrational longer than you can stay solvent."
- You only get one best shot to plan your income right. The shot I am referring to is putting a plan in place to provide the income you will need to live on for the rest of your life.

There is a fountain of youth: it is your mind, your talents, the creativity you bring to your life and the lives of the people you love. When you learn to tap this source, you will have truly defeated age."

—Sophia Loren, actress—

Chapter 6

Ready-Set-Go!

The American iconic author, James Thurber said, "All men should strive to learn before they die what they are running from, and to, and why." Financially speaking, retirement is our home stretch. We want; we need to still have money when we cross the finish line.

So far, our discussion of risk has aimed to deepen your understanding of the losing end of the risk-reward trade-off and its possible effect on your golden years. The purpose is not to teach you that all risk is bad, but to illustrate why it's so important to choose the amount of risk you take, wisely and well—so that losses, when they occur, are not ruinous. The best way to do this in an uncertain world is to determine your risk set point. This is one of the most important investment decisions you can make. Before you can think about what investments you should have in your retirement portfolio, you must know what percentage of your money you can afford to lose, or subject to loss.

To guide you, you first must realize you have your needs to meet and then, after that your lifestyle goals, which dictate where your risk set point should be set. This approach works well because it is so specific. It defines your investment risk in a very personal way. It is based on, and built around your individual needs, lifestyle goals and matched to the specific resources you have. It is not some generic 'theory' or plan we hope works out. In the end, what is our real risk? It is the possibility of falling short of your needs and lifestyle goals. It is the possibility of not being able to maintain your financial independence and dignity for the rest of our life. Risk in retirement is less about the volatility of the assets you hold, than it is about the amount of your assets that are subject to the unknown. The needs/goals driven approach also keeps risk manageable by separating your aspirational wants or lifestyle goals from your fundamental needs, which you cannot afford to place at risk.

In addition to your goals, you also have a distinct personal risk profile to consider and factor into the amount of risk you will ultimately decide upon. Understanding this profile provides the chance to retest your risk set point. And it also serves the second purpose of helping you decide how much of your money you can afford to risk.

How can you bring your risk profile to light? A good approach is to merge the objective view from outside and your subjective judgments from within. Both matter. Ideally, they will complement one another, although this does not always happen. There is considerable debate about whether people have inborn traits that predispose them toward taking or shunning risks, but you don't have to believe that risk preferences are predetermined to discern your individual behavior patterns.

Read on to get a handle on both the objective and subjective sides of your risk profile. As you begin exploring your own risk profile, you may get a more accurate result if you are fortunate to have a financial professional that understands this approach. If you do not or you're not ready for that, maybe you can work through this with your spouse or a friend that knows you well. You will need to choose someone who is not too shy to give you an honest opinion.

Risk is not courage nor is it being bold. To capture you risk profile, let's circle back again to the goals and the lifetime budget we developed in the first part of this book. The markers we've looked at—your goals and your potential lifetime earnings—are also key drivers of your objective risk capacity. How close are you to meeting your income goals? And how much time remains before you must begin to spend from your nest egg assets? Both elements affect how much risk you can take.

As an example, consider the difference between Brandon and Chelsea, ages 64 and 65, a couple I recently met with, and Alexa, who is 60 and single. Both are planning to retire in two years and for the first time thinking about how they will meet their post retirement income needs. After our initial investigation and discussion, it turns out that Alexa will not need to begin using her nest egg assets for eight years after she retires, giving her a ten-year 'income' time horizon. On the other hand, Brandon and Chelsea have a shorter time frame; they will need to utilize some assets immediately upon retiring in two years.

Keep in mind; though they are both retiring in two years, the timing of their income needs is quite different. Alexa has the good fortune of a pension that she will take an eight-year payout for the first eight years of her retirement. This allows her to wait until age 70, when she will file for and get the maximum Social Security worker benefit. Additionally, because she has another ten years, she will be able to take advantage of huge benefit of *compounding her nest egg* for even more additional income, which will replace her pension when it ends. On the other hand, Brandon and Chelsea have much less time and no pensions. They will need to start their Social Security upon retirement and will require a small amount of additional income that will come from their nest egg right away. They both will need to factor inflation into their plan as we will all need more later, as costs rise.

I need to bring special attention to the *compounding of your nest egg* mentioned above. This is very different than the focus most advisors take, which is how to get bigger and better returns. The former provides certainty you can count on; the latter assumes if (highlight on 'IF') you grow a big enough nest egg all will be fine. This is H O P E.

The risk Alexa or Brandon and Chelsea can afford to take is relative to their individual desired level of guarantees or certainty versus potential growth that you 'hope' will coincide with when you need to spend. It is a balance and getting that properly dialed in for your personal situation is the challenge. This can change over time too. In deciding whether to recalibrate risk, it's especially important to keep track of minimal needs. The longer income time horizon you have the more gain you get from compounding when money is properly allocated with a focus on income before growth.

When income is focus one, you place some of your assets in vehicles that provide certainty. They grow and increase your income base whether the market is going up or down, similar to Social Security but they do not have to stop increasing your income at age 70, like Social Security. There are excellent, principal protected fixed annuity products that accomplish this nest egg compounding. If all your assets are at risk (for growth), you risk having less when you need to spend.

Your lifetime income can be flexible or rigid. You may have an occupation, career or business that gives you a post retirement opportunity to work, if you choose. This provides income flexibility. Because flexible income brings hidden growth potential to an individual's earnings power, it allows individuals to take more investment risk. They can partly meet their goals by working more, so flexible earners have greater ability to withstand losses. Their ability to add income through extra work is like a layer of insurance.

For people with no income earning capacity, or those that prefer and choose not to participate in any income earning capacity after retirement have what we call a rigid source of lifetime income. For them, lifetime earnings are relatively fixed and signal a reduced capacity for risk-taking. They have less resilience to losses and need to be more cautious.

Age comes into play, too. People may take greater investment risks when younger, of course. This is not because their holding period is so long, though. Rather, the young have more time to reach their goals. Their future earnings horizon is longer. And, because they typically have more opportunities to change their field of specialization while young, they often have more work flexibility as well.

In considering risk one must be careful to not buy, hook, line and sinker the rationale that is almost always espoused and recommended by Wall Street type advisors which states that even after you retire, you will need to (buy) take market risk for 'growth' because these days you can expect retirement to stretch 20 or even 30 years. According to Wall Street conventional advice, this is long enough to ride out losses, but too long to outlast a safe portfolio with no "growth." That is because they do not know what they do not know. They practice and sell risk for 'growth' and know little or nothing about 'income planning,' especially income planning that provides guarantees which means the money is always there. Even if you have a 25 year plus time horizon for your retirement assets, say 65 to 90, what difference does it make if you need to spend some of that money in 5 or 10 years and it coincides with a big market downturn. This is a retirement killer. You never want to spend money that went down in value. I repeat, you never want to spend money that went down in value.

Most retires plan to live on 'all' their money meaning it is their intention to exhaust their assets. This is a powerful argument against taking a great deal of risk and an argument for providing as much guarantees as you want and need. Guarantees that can last no matter how long you last. That, to me as a Retirement Income Certified Professional, is a much more prudent route.

Once a retirement income plan has been dialed in, it not only makes sense for you to monitor your set point frequently to make sure that you are still comfortable with it, it is necessary if you are to maximize your spendable dollars and live the most life possible. This is best done with a financial professional that thinks things through with you. Together you can test whether you are still comfortable with the plan put together and whether the minimum basic needs relied upon at the outset are working out or not. If not, you can shift your set point and move more money into the safety zone or from the safety zone to the risk category. Income planning is more math and science than art. The hardest part is finding the right help and having realistic conversations. If you can do those two things you will have no problem assembling all these elements into your overall measure for risk capacity. It is also something no professional can do without your help. It must be a team effort. Without your input, discussions and fine-tuning, no plan can be a good plan.

Risk, can you tolerate it? Your ability to take risk is entirely different from how you feel about risk. Risk capacity is an objective measure that reflects how much money you can afford to lose, even in a worst case, without impairing your minimal goals. But how you feel about risk is subjective. It's not necessarily tethered to rational thought. Your risk preference, or tolerance, reflects how willingly you expose yourself to loss in exchange for the possibility of gain. Sometimes referred to as the "sleep factor;" risk tolerance runs the gamut between thrill-seeking behavior and dread. These two measures are equally valid takes on your personal approach to risk. But they ARE NOT equally useful in directing your investment decisions.

It's your risk capacity that sets limits on how much risk you can take. Hand in hand with your goals, risk capacity dictates the size of your safe and risky zones. The constraints that it generates are firm. Your feelings about risk, on the other hand, play a secondary role. This is important to emphasize, because so many popular financial web sites would have your think otherwise. Many of them use a brief attitude quiz to generate an elaborate investment plan, as though your risk tolerance can be gauged on the run and then magically mixed with your time horizon to bake up your ideal asset allocation which is almost always stocks, bonds and/or mutual funds. Both involve risk, by the way. Hmmm?

Where risk preferences become helpful is in your risk category, or Red Money asset allocation. Risk preferences can help guide you to the level of risk that is comfortable, once you know how much of your assets you can take risk with. For some people, whose appetite outstrips his capacity to take risk, knowing your risk preferences is a first step toward taming your animal spirits. On the other hand, you can be more timid than you need to be, and then recognizing your hesitance can help nudge you into a more rational stance when it comes to capacity. Understanding your attitude or preferences towards financial risk can also help you spot and hopefully avoid common behavioral and cognitive mistakes.

It is possible to find some good tests to help determine your risk preferences on the Internet but they are not all good. Typical questions will inquire about your past and present investment behavior, weighing such attitudes as how regretful (or resilient) you are after you lose money. Another good question asks whether you focus on gains or possible losses when you invest. In reality, individuals who evenhandedly consider both possibilities appear to be rare. There are also hypothetical investment scenarios inviting you to specify how much pain you are willing to risk in exchange for different levels of gain.

Questionnaires often ask you to rate yourself on how much risk tolerance you believe you have. Many people answer this question quite accurately, but not everyone gets it right. And tests occasionally weigh psychological traits like skepticism or impulsivity, though separate from your risk tolerance, they can be related. Caution is in order, though, as you review the offerings available to you under the rubric of risk tolerance. Most of the questionnaires circulating on the Web are of dubious quality and reliability. Most experts agree that a test must capture enough information to be reliable. Though a good 6 question risk tolerance quiz is better than a 20 question one that is skewed and asks poor and less relevant questions, a quiz with more good questions is even better.

Other problems with risk questionnaires include a proclivity for irrelevant questions such as queries about circumstances how you 'feel' about risk, marital status, or number of dependents. These questions have no relevancy to your tolerance for risk. Including them produces distortions and worse, information you may incorrectly rely upon or factor into your risk decisions. Another issue stems from the way the questions are presented. As we saw in Chapter 5, framing affects our behavior in subtle but critical ways. Add to this, the fact that we live in a culture that admires risk taking; you can understand why questionnaires can yield biased results. Many respondents, not wanting to appear wimpy, give answers that are insincere. Not good.

There are also risk tolerance questionnaires that ask about your appetite for physical risk, as in, "Do you enjoy jumping out of small airplanes?" This is a test you can toss. Even psychologists who back the proposition that risk tolerance is a stable personality trait have nevertheless concluded that physical and financial risk tolerance are completely different attributes. One does not translate to the other. There are four separate types of risk: Physical, social, ethical, and financial. There is little if any interrelationship among them.

Within the category of financial risk, many analysts have portrayed risk attitudes as stable traits etched deeply into personality. But critics counter that risk preference is a state at any given point in time; it can therefore change depending on current conditions and life experiences. The controversy rolls on. But for us, the results of high quality tests are useful tools either way. The key is to view them in the context of your lifestyle goals and risk capacity and not on their own. When used this way, risk tolerance questionnaires can expose contradictions between risk capacity and risk preference.

And there you have it; a short guide to discovering your own personal risk profile. You are one big step closer toward creating a reliable retirement plan for the right income certainty, tailored for you, balancing the life you want to live for the peace of mind and security you desire, or as we said, "sleep factor."

It's all about the income. A quite important aspect of your financial plan in retirement is knowing your current income needs. As best you can, the next step is your best-educated guesstimate of your future income needs. Consideration and discussion with your financial professional is important to determine when you will have income gaps. Once you have answered these very important questions, you can then find the most efficient and beneficial way to address them, specifically for your individual situation. This will have a very big impact on how you get to live the rest of your life, how much peace of mind you have, how much growth you get from your retirement assets and how much is potentially left at the end of life. Knowing how much you need to live on throughout retirement allows you to discuss with you financial professional, how much of your assets you need to allocate to the protected, 'always going to be there' category. Once this is determined, it will give you the answer to how much you can risk. A key to a successful retirement is being realistic about how much income you will need and the correct asset allocation.

It is better to determine where your income gaps are earlier rather than later. The reason for this is because it is always more cost effective to 'fill' or solve for these gaps earlier than later. You must be aware of them before you can plan to fill them. That is because it allows you to put whatever portion of your retirement nest egg assets to work in the right category, whether for income or for growth. A gap we will all experience is the gap arising from inflation. Most income sources do not have inflation protection, another reason why realistic and accurate planning is needed. Things will cost a lot more in the future; double or even more. In addition to the 'silent killer' income gap created by inflation, other income gaps arise from the death of a spouse, a decrease in Social

Security, the loss of a Social Security check when a spouse dies, the potential loss or ending of a pension, high cost of healthcare, loss of rental income, Medicare changes and costs, to name a few. And, there are almost always unknowns that occur like the need to help a family member and so on.

Every financial strategy for retirement must put the need for regular, dependable income first. I said 'every'. The moment you stop working, your working income ceases, and the paycheck days are over. You begin to live off the money you've worked hard to set aside for retirement. Whether you begin using some of those assets for income right away or not, you have entered the distribution phase of your financial plan. The distribution phase of your retirement plan begins when the earning phase ends. This is when the importance of your Green Money becomes apparent. Do not get side tracked with the term 'Green Money'. We will go into detail on the Color of Money in a later chapter. For now, let it suffice to know Green Money is principal protected and therefore safer and more reliable, designed to provide you with a steady source of income you can depend on. From day one of your retirement for as long as you live, you will need a steady and reliable supply of income. This is provided from your Green Money, the protected money, the 'Know So' money, the money you know will be there. As stated above, meeting that daily income need is about first knowing how much and when you will need it.

How much Income will you need? There is a general rule of thumb that has been floated for many years that states we will need 70 to 80 percent of our pre-retirement income to maintain our lifestyle. But I must say, in my practice, in the real lives of my clients, I have not seen that. Some people plan to travel and do things they have not yet had the opportunity to do, as an example. This will likely cause your income requirement to increase. Just sayin'. For some people, it may be helpful to think of the retirement years in phases; the GO-GO years when you are busy spending money, the SLOW-SLOW years when you slow down and are not as active and the NO-NO years when we can no longer go or do very much, a time when healthcare costs or 'help' care costs rise. Whether your income number is more or less than what you required when working, the challenge is to match your income required with the correct saving and investment strategies; to choose the best options and tools to meet those needs. It is also worth mentioning here that building in flexibility is valuable too. Life almost never unfolds exactly like we anticipate.

When do you need your money? Say you need income immediately, but only for 5 years, until you begin Social Security, as an example. Use the best investment tool to get that specific job done; the job of providing five years of income right away. That will be a different tool than needing additional income if social security gets reduced, say in 2030. You will need a different tool, a different investment product for that. If you need income in the future at some point and you need that to last the rest of your life, find the best investment 'tool' to accomplish that. You are starting to get the idea.

So how do you determine how much you will need and when? Considering costs for all the possibilities; health and 'help' care, potential emergencies, the unknowns, travel, entertainment, helping family, maybe you plan to move, as well as many other retirement expenses, can be a daunting task. The goal is to maximize retirement assets to meet your lifetime income needs. In other words, you need to figure out the best way to 'pensionize' (I want credit for that word in the dictionary, ha!) your assets. This is difficult at best, to accomplish without the help of a retirement planning type financial professional. Particularly, one that is trained and daily focused on the best ways to do that when given a myriad of different scenarios that present themselves.

As was stated earlier, the most important thing you need to do is avoid too much exposure to risk with the assets you need for income. With the help of an income planning type financial professional you get your Green Money and Red Money in order, and together determine the right balance to best and most effectively meet your particular needs. If the market goes down 10% today, or 50% this year, I hope your 'income' needs money is not in that bucket. If so, I hope you like the idea of roommates. I think you should be starting to get the idea that you have to take care of your monthly income needs to pay the bills in retirement as the first order of business. In the next chapter, we will talk about a Green Money source that almost everyone has, the Social Security benefit.

Chapter 6
Takeaways

- Knowing and setting your risk set point is the single most important investment decision you will make. You must know what percentage of your money you can afford to lose before even thinking about what to invest in!
- The basis of a retirement strategy that we can build a solid future on requires us to determine as well as possible how much money we need and when we need it.
- Understanding that most everyone will have income gaps, anticipating them and planning for them, to the best of your ability is integral with retirement peace of mind.
- Risk in retirement is less about the degree of volatility of the assets you hold, than it is about the amount, and the percentage of your assets that are subject to that same volatility. This in a big way will determine if you will be able to maintain your financial independence and dignity for the rest of our life.

"Risk comes from not knowing what you're doing."

—Warren Buffet—

Chapter 7

Safety First

Something major is wrong and most financial professionals either don't know it, or aren't saying! The goal for retirement is how to get the most lifetime satisfaction from the limited amount of financial resources one has. That is putting safety (and reality) first. The safety-first school of thought was originally derived from academic models of how people allocate their resources over a lifetime in order to maximize lifetime satisfaction. Safety-first comes from a more academic foundation, not a sales platform. Therefore, it has been slow to enter the public consciousness because no one is 'selling' it.

The safety-first approach states you must prioritize retirement goals as the first step of developing a good retirement income strategy. If safety is important, a priority, investment strategy must aim to match your individual risk characteristics with the amount of assets you have and the goals you want to accomplish. Prioritizing goals has its academic origins in the idea of utility maximization. Another way of stating it is the more you spend, the less satisfaction you get per dollar. The spending required to satisfy basic needs provides much more value and satisfaction to someone than the additional spending on luxuries after basic needs are met. To make a point: Do you think you would enjoy a fancy car if you were hungry? Retirees should plan to smooth spending over time to avoid overspending on luxuries in one year and being unable to afford necessities later.

The safety-first approach makes funding for what you will need a priority, before the 'extras'. Essential needs are the top priority, then a contingency fund, funds for discretionary expenses, and a legacy fund. It helps to visualize and illustrate retirement funding priorities as a pyramid. Building a retirement strategy requires working from the bottom to properly fund each goal before moving up to the next. The Safety-First pyramid is recreated in Figure 1. There is no consideration for discretionary expenses or providing a legacy until a secure funding source for essential needs and contingencies is in place, to last a lifetime.

Unfortunately, most pre-retirees and retirees will never hear about Modern Retirement Theory as it is presented here. That is because Modern Portfolio Theory and portfolio 'diversification' have been used for many years as the best way to find a suitable balance between investment returns and the volatility of those returns. Money managers, portfolio managers, and investors seek strategies that will support the highest expected growth, subject to the investor's tolerance for loss. What many financial professionals who use this 'theory' to manage the money you need to live on for the rest of your life, do not know is that Modern Portfolio Theory was never meant to apply to the investment problems of families, individuals or retirees. I hope they don't know because if they do and use it anyway, that is much worse.

Nobel laureate and Modern Portfolio Theory founder, Harry Markowitz wrote that Modern Portfolio Theory was developed for large institutions with indefinite lifespans and no specific spending objectives for the portfolio. Meaning, literally that it is a strategy with no end, no exit plan, no income plan, and no way to turn assets safely into income for retirement. There is no spending consideration. HUH! This should be a eureka moment for the entire financial professional retirement industry, but 99% of all financial strategies are still to this day misapplied and utilized even after the author of the theory said it is being used incorrectly. This should be very disconcerting for anyone near retirement.

People are not institutions. They do not live forever. They have finite lifespans. The purpose of saving and investing during the working years is to provide income during retirement. Modern Portfolio Theory does not address this more complicated issue. There is no 'switching of gears' so to speak, for the new terrain. The alternative provided via Modern Retirement Theory is matching your assets with your needs. It focuses more holistically at the level of household needs. In other words, how much do we need to live on now and how much are we likely to need later. It focuses on 'safety' first and therefore strategies that are protected, insured, and for certain. In simple terms, protection of principal and insurance means using guaranteed income type annuities as a solution for longevity and market risk. For many years, before pension money was very deceptively redirected to Wall Street, pensions served a very good purpose. They created income for life! Now you must do that for yourself. In doing so, you are at the mercy of the market, lucky timing, and even, dubious advice. Or... you could take a different route; safety-first.

With this approach, investors are not trying to maximize their year-to-year returns on a risk-adjusted basis, nor are they trying to beat 'the market'. The goal is to have cash flows available to meet spending needs as required, and investments are chosen in such a way that those needs are met with as much certainty as possible and/or... as one desires.

For essential spending, for living expenses, Modern Retirement Theory states that funding must be with assets meeting the criteria of being "secure, stable, and sustainable." Funding options can include Social Security, rental income, pensions, cash value life insurance, and income type annuities. In this regard, another important aspect of the investment approach for the safety-first school is that investing decisions are made in the context of the entire household balance sheet.

This moves beyond looking only at the financial portfolio to consider also the role of human and social capital. Examples of human and social capital include the ability to work part-time, pensions, the social safety net, and so on.

An important point is that volatile assets are inappropriate for basic needs and the contingency fund. Stated again, the objective of investing in retirement is not to maximize risk-adjusted returns, but first to ensure that basics will be covered in any market environment and then to invest the 'rest' for additional potential upside. Riskier assets are suitable for discretionary expenses and legacy, as they will not be needed for the necessities of life.

Asset allocation, therefore, is an output of the analysis, as the entire household balance sheet is used and assets are allocated to match appropriately with the household's liabilities. Matching your assets with your needs removes the probability-based concept of safe withdrawal rates from the analysis, since it rejects relying on a diversified portfolio to pay for your necessities and lifestyle goals.

The idea is to first build a floor of very low-risk, or no risk guaranteed income sources to serve your basic spending needs in retirement. Another way to look at it with the safety-first approach is that you create sufficient pension-like income with your nest egg assets to meet needs. Once there is a sufficient floor in place, you can focus on riskier investments for possible better upside potential. With any remaining assets, you can invest and spend as you wish. Since this extra spending (such as for nice restaurants, extra vacations, etc.) is discretionary, it won't be the end of the world if you must reduce spending at some point. You still have your guaranteed income floor in place to meet your basic needs no matter what happens. With this sort of approach, withdrawal rates are not a concern, and do not really matter.

When it comes to the so-called 'safe withdrawal rate' used by many financial professionals, coming from a diversified portfolio of volatile risk assets, the general view of safety-first advocates is that there is no such thing as a safe withdrawal rate from a volatile portfolio. A truly safe withdrawal rate is unknown and unknowable. Retirees only receive one opportunity to obtain sustainable cash flows from their savings, one chance to do it right—and they must develop a strategy that will meet basic needs no matter the length of life or the sequence of post-retirement market returns and inflation.

Retirees have little leeway for error. Returning to the labor force might not be a realistic option. Volatile assets like stocks, mutual funds and even bonds in our current interest rate climate that (might) or might not last the rest of our lifetime are not appropriate when seeking to meet basic retirement living expenses. Just because a strategy did not fail over a particular historical period does not ensure it will not fail in your financial future. There is a reason they call these 'safe' withdrawal rate calculations coming out of volatile assets *Monte Carlo simulations.*

I think it is important enough to repeat: The objective for retirement is to first build a safe and secure income floor for the rest of your life. Only after that should you include more volatile assets that may provide greater upside potential for the price of the additional risk. In terms of this floor for essentials and contingencies, it is Social Security, rental income, pensions, and income annuities that should take the lead. Failure should not be an option when meeting basic needs. If you do not have sufficient guaranteed sources like Social Security, pension, rental income, etcetera to meet your basic needs, then income annuities can serve as a fundamental building block for retirement income. Your IRA, 401(k) type assets get converted to guaranteed income. When done properly this is income that will last the rest of your life.

Income annuities are especially valuable because of their ability to provide longevity protection through the provision of mortality credits. People do not know their age of death in advance. They can learn about their remaining life expectancy, and they can have an informed opinion, but that is just a projection of the average outcome and there is a surprisingly large distribution of actual lifespans around the average. Individual retirees cannot self-insure to protect themselves from living too long. This is what insurance companies do, using annuities.

The annuity provider, however, can pool longevity risk across a large group of retirees, with mortality credits. It is complicated but easy to understand if you compare it to homeowner's insurance as an example. They can replace your home at a cost of $500,000 even though you only pay $1,000 for homeowner's insurance. They can do that by 'pooling' all homeowner assets. Because the annuity provider can pool the longevity risk, they can make payments at a rate much closer to what would be possible when planning for remaining life expectancy.

A retiree seeking to self-insure must assume a time horizon extending well beyond life expectancy; thirty years or more using a guesstimated percentage with no certainty if it will work or not. A cautious retiree would have to be very careful to spend less when self-insuring against a long life than if they have 'insured' or guaranteed income.

Chapter 7
Takeaways

- 1. Retirement is an absolute goal, not a relative one.
- 2. Planning needs to be individualized and client-centric. For income and security, planning and executing retirement funding should focus on individuals rather than historical data or group statistics.
- 3. Outlook ambiguity—the future is unknowable to the individual. Modern Retirement Theory acknowledges that future events are always unknown to individuals.
- 4. Modern Retirement Theory provides retirement income that is simultaneously secure, stable and sustainable for life.
- 5. Retirement income planning looks at all assets and all expenses, including inflation that will affect the retiree. Modern Retirement Theory states that the best way to plan for as much certainty as possible is to utilize an individual's entire balance sheet, not just his or her portfolio, as well as off-balance sheet items like Social Security, pensions, rental income, etc. In other words, one must consider their entire lifetime picture, all their assets, and all their potential needs together.
- 6. A hierarchical priority of retirement funding should be established to offset retirement risk. By funding for the things that provide the most satisfaction and security; in other words the essentials, retirees gain the most satisfaction as well as the ability to take risk with the money they do not need to provide those essentials.

> *"The secret to financial security is not to have more money, but having more control over the money we presently have."*
>
> —Auliq-Ice—

Chapter 8

Building Your Retirement Pyramid—Social Security

As we know, pyramids must be built with a solid, strong foundation. It will be required to hold a great weight. In the case of your retirement, that foundation must support the weight of your financial security, peace of mind, and ultimately, your retirement happiness. This is the rest of your life and there are no re-dos. The foundation of your retirement pyramid must be built with money that you know will be there for you to live on. The foundation is made up of assets you will use early in retirement as well as later, for income. This money we think of as our 'Know So' money. It is the money we 'know' will be there for us, the money we will be able to count on. This can include pensions, rental income, annuities, cash value life insurance, and Social Security. Sorry to be repetitive, but I am trying to balance what you have heard for 30 years. For most Americans, one source that retirees will have as part of their nest egg assets to rely on for income is Social Security. It is or will be an important part of your retirement income. It is not just a matter of deciding when to take it, and you should realize that Social Security should not be considered as a standalone asset decision. Yes, Social Security is one of your assets. To convert your Social Security asset into the maximum spendable dollars it must be considered with all of your other retirement assets. As we have previously learned, properly managing assets for retirement is different. It is no longer the working years. The first thing you and your financial professional should consider when creating your income plan is your Social Security benefit options. Social Security is the foundation of income planning for anyone who is about to retire and is a reliable source in your overall income plan. Making the 'best' possible decision vs. the wrong one can cost you tens, even hundreds of thousands of dollars in lost retirement income.

I recently met with a potential 64-year-old new client who had worked full-time for most of his life and planned to retire in one year at age 65. He was looking forward to enjoying retirement with his wife, children and grandkids. They were looking at RVs and were going to do some traveling, seeing places they had been putting on their list for years. When he turned 62, he decided to take advantage of his Social Security benefits as soon as they became available. Like many people, he was afraid benefits might not be there for him later; so he figured he better get them early before they were gone.

Now several years later, discussing the issue in my office, as we looked at his Social Security statement he began to have doubts about the decision he made previously, and maybe prematurely. I told him that I was confident Social Security would be there for him to count on. Also, because he continued to work and collect his Social Security benefits, his Social Security was reduced one dollar for every two dollars he earned over the earnings limit for his age. That meant that he only received half of what he would have received if he had not continued to work while collecting his benefit. I mean, since we worked for it, we earned the benefit, why should we get penalized further for taking it early? Furthermore, when I told him that if he had waited to age 66 his benefits check would have been 25% greater, and if he had waited until age 70 it would increase by another 32%, making his benefit a total of 65% greater for the rest of his life. I know; 25 plus 32 does not equal 65. The math is off because it is compounded. Oh, and that much larger check would have been his wife's after he is gone, since the remaining spouse gets the larger of the benefits whether it is their own or the spouses. The clincher was that he did not even need the income; he was still working. Yikes. So, in retrospect that was for his situation, a poor and costly decision on several fronts. One that could not be undone.

Some facts about Social Security benefits and retirees using them:

- 90 percent of Americans, age 65 and older receive Social Security benefits.
- Social Security provides 40 percent of income required for the average household. Are you average? How much of your required needs will it pay?

- Claiming Social Security benefits at the wrong time can reduce your monthly benefit by as much as 65 percent.
- 43% of men and 48% of women claim Social Security benefits at age 62. For most of them it turns out to be a mistake, usually based on bad information and things they have 'heard' but not verified.
- Unfortunately, 74% of retirees receive less than full Social Security benefits.
- In 2013, the average monthly Social Security benefit was $1,261. The maximum benefit for 2013 was $2,533. The $1,272 monthly benefit reduction between the average and the maximum is applied forever; meaning, the rest of one's life. That is a lot of money.

I want to be very clear; I am not saying it is always best to wait. NO, every situation is different. No two retirees have the same assets, income sources, anticipated longevity, or life scenarios. All of these factors and more need to be considered carefully.

Many aspects of Social Security are well known and there are others that are not. When it comes time for you to begin collecting on your Social Security benefit there are many options and choices. There are hundreds of claiming combinations and thousands of calculations necessary to best analyze someone's benefit. Social Security is a massive government program that manages retirement benefits for millions of people. It is also changing as I write this. There are experts that spend their entire careers understanding and analyzing Social Security. Luckily, you don't have to understand all of the intricacies of Social Security to maximize the benefits. You simply need to know where to go to get the needed help. There is software that income type planners utilize that does all the calculations. That is then used to intelligently interpret your situation, sufficiently discuss the issues, and factor all that into a plan with everything else you have. The software does not make decisions; it provides great information so that you, together with your financial professional, can make the best decisions. You need to know exactly what to do to get the most from your Social Security benefit and when to do it. Taking the time to create a roadmap for your Social Security strategy will help ensure that you efficiently coordinate it with the rest of your assets and get the most from your benefit.

Though you don't control how much you put into Social Security, and you don't control what it's invested in or how the government manages it (or mismanages it, more appropriately), you do control when and how you file for benefits. The question we all think about regarding Social Security that needs to be answered is, "When should I start taking Social Security?" Before we can answer this very important and pressing question, before you can discuss it, there are a couple of key pieces of information you need to have. This takes a little bit of work.

Before we get into a few calculations and strategies that can make all the difference, let's start by covering the basic information about Social Security which should give you an idea of where you stand. Before we do though, let me say that, like a well built home, your retirement plan must be built upon a strong foundation. For many retirees that starts with Social Security. Just like concrete requires a strong and dependable formula (rock mainly), the base; the foundation of your retirement plan needs a strong and dependable ingredient also, that would be… GUARANTEES. Social Security includes that in the formula. It provides a guarantee, security and (some) peace of mind. The purpose of the information that follows is not to provide a complete and detailed explanation of how Social Security works, as that would be a book bigger than this one. The intention is to give you some tools sufficient for you to begin asking some questions so you can start to understand how Social Security affects your retirement and how you can begin to prepare for making some of those decisions.

Eligibility is where we begin. Understanding how and when you are eligible for Social Security benefits helps to clarify what to expect when the time comes to claim them. To receive retirement benefits from Social Security, you must be eligible, or as it is properly stated you must earn eligibility. In almost all cases, Americans born after 1929 must earn 40 quarters of credit to be eligible to draw their Social Security retirement benefit. In 2013, one Social Security credit was earned in any calendar quarter you earned $1,160. The number changes since it is indexed each year, but it does not change much. For comparison in 2012, a credit represented $1,130 earned in a calendar quarter. Four quarters of credit is the maximum number that can be earned each year. To accumulate four credits in 2013, a worker would have to earn at least $4,640. In order to qualify for retirement benefits, you must have earned a minimum number of credits. Additionally, if you are at least 62 years old and have been married to a recipient of Social Security benefits for at least 12 months, you can choose to receive Spousal benefits.

Primary Insurance Amount or PIA, represents the amount of your Social Security benefit you will receive at your Full Retirement Age, aka FRA. Your benefit amount at your FRA, and will neither reduce nor increase due to early or delayed retirement options. However, if you opt to take benefits before your FRA, your monthly benefit will be less than your Primary Insurance Amount. Your lifetime benefit base will be locked in at a lesser amount. On the other hand, waiting until after your FRA to access your benefits will increase your benefit beyond your PIA. However, you also must consider every month you wait is one less check you get over your lifetime.

Full Retirement Age. Your FRA is an important figure for anyone who is planning to rely on Social Security benefits in their retirement. Depending on when you were born, there is a specific age at which you will attain FRA. Your FRA is determined by the year you were born and is the age at which you can begin your full monthly benefit. Your FRA is important because it is half of the equation used to calculate your Social Security benefit. The other half of the equation is based on when you start taking benefits. It seems that the way this is determined makes it more complicated. Since it is all based on FRA, you either receive less than your primary insurance amount if you take it sooner or you receive more if you wait beyond FRA.

When Social Security was initially set up, the FRA was age 65, and it still is for people born before 1938. But as time has passed the age for receiving full retirement benefits has increased. Some people consider this unfair but the average age of death was 65 in 1938. If you were born between 1938 and 1960, your full retirement age is somewhere on a sliding scale between 65 and 67 (see below).

Anyone born in 1960 or later will now have to wait until age 67 for full benefits. Increasing the FRA has helped the government reduce the cost of the Social Security program, which pays out more than a half trillion dollars to beneficiaries every year, with more and more baby boomers retiring every day.

While you can begin collecting benefits as early as age 62, the amount you receive, as a monthly benefit will be less than it would be if you wait until you reached your FRA. It is important to note and reiterate: If you file for Social Security benefit before your FRA, the reduction to your monthly benefit will last for the rest of your life. You can also delay receiving benefits up to age 70, in which case your benefits will be higher than your PIA for the rest of your life.

- At FRA, 100 percent of PIA is available as a monthly benefit.
- At age 62, your Social Security retirement benefits are available. For each month you take benefits prior to your FRA, however, the monthly amount of your benefit is reduced. This reduction stays in place for the rest of your life.
- At age 70, your monthly benefit reaches its maximum. After you turn age 70, your monthly benefit will no longer increase.

Year of birth	Full Retirement Age
1943-1954	66
1955	66 and 2 months
1956	66 and 4 months
1957	66 and 6 months
1958	66 and 8 months
1959	66 and 10 months
1960 or later	67*

It's all about the 'roll up', and we are not talking 'jelly'! Your Social Security income 'rolls up' the longer you wait to claim it. Your monthly benefit will continue to increase until you turn 70 years old. From age 62 through FRA (Full Retirement Age, 66 for most of us (see above), you get an approximate 6% per year guaranteed 'roll up'. OH, and it is compounded! This is no small matter. That means your Social Security income base is going to increase your income by about 6% each year, compounded (did I tell yah?). So, if your Social Security income at age 62 is $1,500, at age 66 (for most of us) it will be about $1,894. From Full Retirement Age (66 for most) until you are 70 your guaranteed 'roll up' is about 8% per year, compounded. Using the same scenario as above, at age 70 your monthly benefit check would be approximately $2,576. An interesting and eye opening fact though; only 4 percent of Americans wait until after their FRA to file for their benefits. Every dollar you increase your Social Security income by means less money you must spend from your nest egg to meet your retirement income needs later and yet most people do not wait beyond their FRA. Many, as I said before take it even earlier. For many people, creating their Social Security strategy is the most important decision they can make to positively impact their retirement. The difference between the best and worst Social Security decision can be tens of thousands of dollars over a lifetime of benefits. In some cases, a couple of hundred thousand!

NOW or **LATER?** We are not talking about candy here. OK, it seems simple, right? Wrong! Nothing about retirement planning is simple and that for sure includes Social Security claiming. Following the above logic, it makes sense to wait as long as you can to begin receiving your Social Security benefit. However, the answer isn't always that simple. Not everyone has the option of waiting. Many people need to rely on Social Security on day one of their retirement. In fact, nearly 50 percent of 62-year-old Americans file for Social Security benefits at age 62. Why is this number so high? Some might need the income. Others might be in poor health and don't feel they will live long enough to make FRA worthwhile for themselves or their families. But the truth is however, that the majority of folks taking an early benefit at age 62 are simply under-informed about Social Security. Perhaps they make this major decision based on rumors and emotion.

Longevity must be factored in too. The longer you wait, the less years you get paid. You absolutely must take all assets and anticipated longevity into the consideration and decision. As stated previously, Social Security is not a standalone decision. You must look at your entire asset and goals scenario. One of the reasons is that you don't just need help; you need help from someone that is in sync with and is experienced with this understanding. As a reminder, the biggest part and the foundation of retirement planning is not about returns; it's about the income, and how to get the most income from the asset growth you have already gotten. Hopefully.

Some reasons you may want to file early is that you find your job unbearable; you may see the 'extra' life lived more valuable than the additional money gained by working; or maybe you are not healthy and need a reliable source of income. Some reasons you might consider delaying your benefit are that you want to maximize your Social Security income; you want to increase retirement benefits for your spouse, you enjoy your work and can still do it, or you are healthy and anticipate living a long time.

So, if you decide to wait, how long should you wait? Lots of people can put it off for a few years, but not everyone can wait until they are 70 years old. Your individual circumstances will play a big part in determining when you should begin taking Social Security. If you do the math, you will quickly see that between ages 62 and 70, there are 96 months in which you can file for your Social Security benefit. If you take into account those 96 months and the 96 months your spouse could also file for Social Security, and the number of different strategies for structuring your benefit, you can easily end up with more than 20,000 different scenarios. It's safe to say this isn't the kind of math that you can easily do at home. Each month would result in a different benefit amount. The longer you wait, the higher your monthly benefit amount becomes. Each month you wait, however, is one less month that you receive a Social Security check.

Maximizing your lifetime benefits may not always mean waiting until you can get the largest monthly payment. If you know that every month you wait, your Social Security benefit goes up a little bit, and you also know that every month you wait, you receive one less benefit check, how do you determine where the sweet spot is that maximizes your benefits over your lifetime? Income planning type financial professionals have access to software that will calculate the best year and month for you to file for benefits based on your default, or actuarial life expectancy. You can further customize that information by estimating your life expectancy based on your health, habits and family history. Then you must create an income plan (we'll discuss this later) that helps you wait until the target date for you to file for Social Security for your specific situation. This is how you can optimize your retirement income strategy to get the most out of your benefit. Regarding your life expectancy, I think you have a better idea than the government does. They rely on averages to make their calculations. You have much more personal information about your health, lifestyle and family history than they do. You can use that knowledge to potentially increase your lifetime benefit.

While you can and should educate yourself about how Social Security works, the reality is you don't need to know all the intricacies of Social Security to make choices about your retirement. What you do need to know is the best decision to maximize your benefit. For many people, it can represent the largest portion of their retirement income. Not treating your Social Security benefit as one of your retirement assets along with any and all your other assets can lead to significantly under optimizing one of your largest sources for retirement income.

Working with the 'right' financial professional, one who makes income optimization their specialty is often the key to Optimizing Social Security benefits. Here is an example:

Brian and Darlene Repasy are a typical American couple that have worked their whole lives and saved when they could. When they came to see us, Brian was 60 years old, and Darlene was 56 years old. They sat down with us to determine their PIAs. Brian's PIA was $1,910 and Dar's was $921.

If the Repasy's retire at age 62 and begin taking retirement benefits from Social Security, they will receive an estimated $492,000 in lifetime benefits. That may seem like a lot, but if you divide that amount over 20 years, it averages out to be just shy of $25,000 per year. The Repasys are accustomed to a more significant annual income than that. To make up the difference, they will have to rely on alternative retirement income options for the additional money needed. They will need to depend on their nest egg, their 401(k) and IRA assets. If they wait until their FRA they will increase their lifetime benefits to an estimated $615,000. This option will provide them a $30,750 annual income vs. $25,000.

After learning the Repasy's needs and using software to calculate the most optimal time to begin drawing benefits, we were then able to use that along with the information about their other sources and assets to discuss and determine that the best option for them greatly increased their potential lifetime benefits to $701,800! Their best decision, based on all the facts did not have them waiting until 70, as about 67 1/2 was optimum.

By using strategies that were recommended, they increased their potential lifetime benefits by more than $209,000. There's no telling how much you could miss out on if you don't make time to create a strategy that calculates your maximum benefit. For the Repasys, the value of maximizing their benefits was the difference between a life of security and confidence vs. one of cutting back, concern and worry.

While this may seem like a special case, it isn't uncommon to find benefit increases of this magnitude. You'll never know unless you take a serious look at your own options with your financial professional. Before you pick up the phone and call Social Security Administration (SSA), you should know that the Social Security Administration representatives are prohibited from giving you election advice. Plus, SSA representatives in general are trained to focus on monthly benefit amounts, not the lifetime income for a family. More importantly they know nothing about how to coordinate Social Security with all your other assets.

As discussed previously, calculating how to maximize lifetime benefits is more important than waiting until age 70 for your biggest check. Remember, it's about getting the most income during your lifetime! That is the goal for most retirees. Professional benefit maximization software can target the year and month that it is most beneficial for you to file based on your life expectancy but it is your individual situation, what other assets you have and having the right discussions that will maximize your lifetime income. Your Social Security options don't stop here, however. There are other considerations that can also manipulate your benefit payments for increase. Here are a few.

The **Retired Worker Benefit** is the benefit that most people are familiar with. The Retired Worker Benefit is what we have been talking about. When we talk about our Social Security benefit it is the Retired Worker Benefit. It is your benefit based on your earnings and the amount that you have paid into the system over the span of your career.

The **Spousal Benefit** is available to the spouse of someone who is eligible for Retired Worker Benefits. There may be a way for your spouse to receive a check from your benefit and not lose the chance to get his or her maximum benefit when he or she turns age 70. Many people do not know about this strategy and might be missing out on benefits they have earned.

The **Survivorship Benefit.** When one spouse passes away, the survivor can receive the larger of the two benefit amounts.

What we know as **File and Suspend** as a benefit claiming strategy has ceased to exist as a result of the Bipartisan Budget Act passed in October 2015. This claiming option involved one spouse, usually the higher earner but not always, opening their record for benefits but immediately suspending payment. The purpose was to allow the worker's spouse to begin a spousal benefit while the worker's benefit continued to earn delayed retirement credits on his own record. A catch to the new legislation is that when a client suspends his benefit, all benefits paid from his record are also suspended. Previously, a beneficiary could suspend benefits while a spouse and young children could continue collecting a benefit from his record.

The new legislation will also require that a beneficiary be receiving his or her own benefit in order for other benefits to be paid from his record. The new legislation does leave on the table the ability to suspend benefits for the purpose of accruing delayed retirement credits. So, if you have filed early and now believe it was a mistake, you can suspend benefits and continue to accrue delayed retirement credits from that point until you retake your benefit.

The other major change with the passage of new rules is the elimination of the **Restricted Application.** Restricted application allowed a spouse who had attained full retirement age, who was also eligible for his or her own retirement benefit, to collect only a spousal benefit. At a later date, usually age 70, the spouse would switch to his or her own retirement benefit, which would have grown to its maximum with delayed retirement credits.

The new legislation extends a concept called **Deemed** Filing.

Deemed filing has only been a factor before reaching full retirement age. Prior to reaching full retirement age, if a client filed for any benefit, he or she was "deemed to be filing" for all benefits. This meant that if a client was eligible for his or her own benefit and a spousal benefit, he or she would only be paid a single benefit—the equivalent of the higher of the two. But if the individual waited until full retirement age to claim a benefit, he or she could choose which benefit to receive. If the choice were made to receive a spousal benefit, his or her own retirement benefit would continue to accrue delayed retirement credits. The new rule extends the deemed filing provision to age 70, meaning that it's now impossible to choose which benefit to claim and that the payable benefit will always be the higher benefit if eligible for more than one. There is one not so small concession in the new legislation that we find interesting. The new rules around restricted application apply only to individuals who attain age 62 after 2015. For those who achieve age 62 prior to 2016, it remains possible to file a restricted application for spousal benefits only at full retirement age. However, this option is being effectively "phased out" over the next four years.

Voluntary Suspension still exists. For clients who claimed benefits early, it remains possible for them to stop their benefits at full retirement age for the purpose of earning delayed retirement credits. This may be useful for clients who begin benefits early, but for some reason change their minds. An example is, you are forced to retire, and taking your worker benefit becomes necessary, then you get a new job and do not need the Social Security. Voluntarily suspending will allow their benefit to earn delayed retirement credits until age 70. Just note that voluntarily suspending the benefit will also stop any other benefits paid to family members.

Widows Benefits remain unchanged. It will still be possible for a widow to begin a widow benefit and switch to his or her own retirement benefit at a later date, or vice versa.

The 'D' factor. How does a divorced spouse qualify for benefits? If you have gone through a divorce, it might affect the retirement benefit to which you are entitled. A person can receive benefits as a divorced spouse on a former spouse's Social Security record if he or she: Was married to the former spouse for at least 10 years; Is at least age 62 years old; Is unmarried; and is not entitled to a higher Social Security benefit on his or her own record. It is worth noting that divorced benefits seem to have suffered what some are calling an unintended consequence of the legislation. As of now, since filing a restricted application will not be available for anyone reaching age 62 after 2015, divorced individuals will not able to use this option unless they fall into the grandfathered group who will already be aged 62 by the end of 2015.

With all the different options, strategies and benefits to be considered, you can see why filing for Social Security is more complicated than just completing the paperwork. Gathering the data and educating yourself sufficiently so that you are aware of all your different options and make the right choices means a lot. You can knock yourself out trying to figure out which options are best, and you can take educated guesses as to how to coordinate with all your other assets but you still be wondering if you made the best decisions. Another option is to work with a financial professional, an income planning type professional who uses customized software that takes all the variables of Social Security and, just as or more important all the specifics and variables of your specific situation into account. As mentioned before, there are thousands of different filing options for your Social Security benefit. If married, the options increase; the bigger age difference there is, the more consideration is required too. This is far more complicated arithmetic than most people can do by themselves. If you want to truly and accurately understand the when and how to file, you are going to need someone who will ask you the right questions about your situation, and have the necessary discussions. It will be someone who has access to specialized software that can crunch the numbers and bring it all together. The reality is that you need to work with a professional that can provide you with the sophisticated analysis of your situation, so you can make informed decisions. They are the only kind of decisions that can provide peace of mind. Again, a full and total discussion on Social Security and the coordination of that with all your other assets and other issues too (like Medicare, Required Minimum Distributions, and Social Security taxation, to name a few) is not possible here.

Chapter 8
Takeaways

- To get the most out of your Social Security benefit, you need to file at the right time, for you, for your specific situation. The longer you wait, the bigger the check. The sooner you claim benefits, the more checks you get.
- If you have other assets (and I hope you do), you must consider them together and coordinate the spending of those assets along with your Social Security claiming decision. That is the only way to maximize your hard-earned money for maximum income in retirement and for legacy; another issue with no room to discuss here.
- There is way too much riding on the 'right' decisions. Don't try this at home. The people working at the SSA cannot help you in coordinating these decisions.

*"Money is hard to earn and easy to lose.
Guard yours with care."*

—Brian Tracy—

Chapter 9

Build Your Foundation To Last

As previously mentioned, in addition to Social Security, the foundation, the biggest most important part of your retirement pyramid can also be structured with income from other sources. These include, but are not limited to pensions, rental income, annuities, and cash value life insurance. As we think about these other sources there is one issue, a big issue. If you do not already have a pension, net rental income or cash value life insurance, you are not likely to establish those as sources now. Therefore, they are very likely not options. That leaves us with annuities. If you are one of those that have a 'conditioned' sense of anxiety about annuities, you will need to work harder at overcoming that if you want additional income security. Education is the answer. An annuity is simply a financial tool; that is all. If it happens to be the 'best' tool to fix a retirement problem, handle an issue you have, one of needing and/or wanting more guaranteed income, more income certainty in life, then an annuity is a tool you will need to get better acquainted with. Keep in mind, if they fix your problem or solve your issue, you do not need to love annuities; you do not even need to like annuities. I mean, do you love the hammer in your toolbox? Probably not. But, if you need to drive a nail, you use it anyway, right? It is the best tool for that job.

Annuities may be the only other source of additional guaranteed income available to almost everyone. If you have a pension, then you already have an annuity. Even if you do not have a pension, if you did you would have an annuity. It is an annuity. There is no shortage of controversy, bias, lack of knowledge and therefore confusion regarding annuities. This is something we will work through as best we can here. The Media, the Wall Street talking heads and most financial advisors generally make negative comments about annuities. That attitude comes from one of two places. It is either a lack of real knowledge about how they work, what they do and the security that only an annuity can provide or from something worse. That 'worse' is a self-serving desire to sell you what they have; the risk type investments, the 'hope so' type of investments whether that is good for you in retirement or not. I will not belabor this point, but it is a big one.

There is nothing better for converting retirement assets into income certainty. Studies have proven that having the additional guaranteed source of lifetime income will make your portfolio last longer and eliminate the risk of running out of money. The reason is, if income planning is done right, using guaranteed sources for the foundation of your retirement pyramid; you will not need to live out of a portfolio that has lost value. Remember, spending money that has gone down in value only serves to compound loss and risk. Not good! Having annuities in effect lengthens the time horizon on your risk assets as your income needs are met with guarantees. In effect, it makes the risk you decide to take, less risky because your needs are met with guarantees.

One reason annuities are controversial is because all types of annuities are almost always lumped together when being discussed. This creates a great deal of misinformation and the misinformation creates the confusion. I mean a Yugo and a Maserati are both cars but that is where the similarity ends, right? Annuities are like that too. They may all be annuities but so very different and yet they are spoken about and discussed like there is just one type, like they are all the same and work the same. Nothing could be further from the truth. The confusion ends up seeming like a lack of transparency and then we are suspicious. Education and clarity are the answer. Many annuities have high fees, inherent risk and require one to give up assets in exchange for income. If that isn't problem enough, most people have not had a good experience buying annuities. Most people buy annuities the wrong way because they are not given any other option. They have contact with an agent/advisor who presents a specific annuity. They then decide whether or not to put money into that annuity and how much. That is completely backwards. First you must determine what your income requirement is now and as best you can, for the rest of your life. The next step is to determine how much of that income you want guaranteed vs. much of it you are willing to be unsure of. Then you must find the help of a good financial professional you trust to help you do the heavy lifting; someone who can do income planning and has experience researching the right annuity for each situation.

On top of the above, oftentimes one's experience can be negative because many advisors do not understand how income annuities truly work and/or they sell what they have instead of doing the hard work of 'income planning'. They do not do the in-depth work necessary to be sure the right annuity is utilized for the particular situation and individuals' requirements. They typically use talking points to 'sell' the annuity instead of education and collaboration to put together solutions that last a lifetime.

I think every retiree needs to know enough about annuities, even if in the end, they don't need one. You must know more in order to determine if it is something you should consider as part of an overall plan for your retirement, or not. So, let's get started by learning some basics about annuities.

ANNUITIES- The Good, Bad and Ugly

An annuity is a contract between you and an insurance company in which you make a lump sum payment or series of payments and in return obtain regular disbursements beginning either immediately or at some point in the future. Also, they can be used for protected growth that goes to beneficiaries. This is happening more frequently today too. The term **annuity** refers to two very different types of legal contracts with very different purposes. By tradition, the term annuity referred to what is more appropriately referred to nowadays as an **immediate annuity.** This is an insurance contract which makes a series of either level or fluctuating payments, paid out over a fixed number of years or during the lifetime(s) of one or two individuals, or in one of many combinations of the two lifetimes as well as a period of certain guaranteed options, such as 10, 15, or 20 years. The characteristic of the immediate annuity is that it is a vehicle used for distributing money saved for retirement. It is a vehicle designed for when it is time to switch from maximizing growth to maximizing what you will be able to spend. A common use, for an immediate annuity is to provide pension income to a person who is due to retire. As mentioned above, this is the way it used to be prior to the inception of the 401(k). This type of annuity has no up-front fees, no annual fees or other costs as they are calculated into the equation before your promised income amount is set. As a Retirement Income Certified Professional, generally speaking I do not use immediate annuities, as it requires you to give up your money in exchange for income. I always think options and flexibility are better and to me, keeping your money and... getting the income you need is a much better solution.

Another application for the term annuity came into being in the 1970s. This is generally identified as a **deferred annuity** and it is a vehicle for accumulating savings as well as building up an income base for guaranteed income later. This differs from the immediate annuity and causes confusion when people discuss annuities without carefully defining which type of annuity they have in mind.

Annuities are becoming one of the financial industry's fastest growing products, with annual sales of domestic annuities for 2013 being more than $65 billion in the U.S. alone. It was reported in the Treasury Department report on the insurance industry for 2012 that there was more than $339 Billion in annuity deposits. As one can see the interest is snow balling. As more and more baby boomers convert from their working years to their spending, retirement years, this trend will only continue to increase.

Annuities come in numerous classifications, types, and versions. While annuities are not for everyone they are likely appropriate for anyone that cannot take another hit like 2008 and lose 50% or for those that just prefer not to lose sleep over stock market volatility for the rest of their days.

Before 1985, before 401(k)s, if you had a reasonably decent job, you likely had a pension plan as part of your earnings. Technically, it was likely a defined pension benefit plan. A defined pension benefit plan is a plan in which an employer/sponsor promises a specified monthly benefit on retirement that is predetermined by a formula based on the employee's earnings history, tenure of service and age, rather than depending directly on individual investment returns. Traditionally, many governmental and public entities, as well as many corporations, provided defined benefit plans, sometimes as a means of compensating workers in lieu of increased pay. A defined benefit plan is 'defined' in the sense that the benefit formula is defined and known in advance. It was about how much income you would retire with, not how much money. After all, it is income we need to live on. Yes, income comes from money; but if you are chasing growth solely via a volatile stock market, you will never know how much income you will have. That is because you cannot know how much money you will have in any given year. Your income is at the mercy of the market.

The gist of pension was that as part of your compensation, the employer would put aside money for you and when you retired, they would give that sum of money to an insurance company and the insurance company would provide you the 'pension'; otherwise known as 'income for the rest of your life'. That was and is an ANNUITY. Unfortunately, today pensions for the most part have gone the way of the dinosaur. Some of you reading this book, those 55 years and older may still have a pension that will be part of your retirement income. If you do, congratulations, but you are in the minority. I will avoid the soapbox here and just get to the point. Once companies figured out that 401(k)s took much of the responsibility and the liability of providing for employees after retirement and put it squarely in the laps of the employees, there was no going back.

Up until that time, annuities in the form of pensions played a very large roll in securing workers' income for retirement. Oh, and it worked very well. People knew how much they would have and they could make a plan for their life during retirement. Unfortunately, something very sneaky, and in my mind, devious began to happen. Simultaneously with the winding down of pensions and the inception of 401(k)s, Wall Street, in conjunction with our legislators for all intents and purposes gave us only once place to grow that 401(k) money while we continued to work. And that was in the market... at risk. No pension building, principal protected options.

Think about this for a minute; prior to 1986, how many people were investors? Did your parents invest? Your grandparents? Before that time most people that had money, that we knew, they 'saved'. That is how they accumulated their money; they saved it.

Now, think about this, let's say that you are a gambler, a Wild West gambler like Brett Maverick, Wyatt Earp, Batt Masterson or a John Henry 'Doc' Holiday. You like to play for big stakes; no penny ante stuff. Let's say you play with the same five or six people regularly. No matter how much money all of you have combined, the stakes are limited by the amount everyone has, right? Not only are the stakes limited but it is a situation of, one night you win another night someone else wins. You are just taking, winning, if you will, each other's money back and forth. Now, imagine the most creative one at the table, I am guessing it is Maverick, figures out a way to, maybe not to force other people to play their 'game', but a way to make them seem like they were idiots if they didn't. I mean, like maybe, they tell you, "Hey, if you get some money in the 'game', on the table, we will actually put some in for you too. We will match what you put in up to a certain amount." Then they let you know that Uncle Sam even likes you playing the 'game'. So much so that they will allow you to postpone paying any income taxes on the money you put into the 'game'. They even make it seem like even if you don't know how to play, you are still going to make money. "Just do what we tell you, you'll be fine." Is this starting to sound a bit silly? Or, is it starting to sound a bit familiar?

Did you know that by 1985 the amount of money in the 'game', invested in the stock market was never more than $2,301,000,000 ($2.3 Billion) and only a short 15 years later that amount had jumped to an enormous $15,108,000,000,000.1 (15.108 Trillion) Why? Because of all the baby boomers that got into the Wall Street poker 'game'. Oh, and today it is almost double that as of this writing. Question: Do you think the game was set up for you, for you to make money or do you just think it was… a 'set up'? Hmmm? I do know that it is beyond interesting that prior to that time, before pensions went away, insurance companies 'insured' retirees' futures. After that there was no option for employees to let insurance companies do what they had always done, which was to provide a lifetime income annuity, otherwise known as, a pension.

Today, more and more astute pre-retirees and retirees are

learning that they can do for themselves what their company 401(k) plan administrators would not do for them. They can go direct to the insurers and provide their own pension, in the form of an annuity with a Guaranteed Income Benefit. There will be more on this later.
1. Some of this difference is market growth, but it does not change the fact that prior to the 401(k), most middle-income families did not take risk (in the stock market).

Some of the reasons 55 and uppers like annuities are;
- More growth potential when associated with a market index
- There is no tax payable on accumulated interest as it continues to grow and compound tax deferred
- An individual has the ability to develop an income with 100% tax dollars or taxable dollars, or even tax free dollars, like a ROTH IRA
- Annuities protect your principal; a very key consideration for pre-retirees and retirees
- Annuities come with guarantees, including minimum rates of return, if the market does poorly
- The tax on Social Security can be reduced or eliminated for some period by the use of deferred annuities
- The proceeds payable upon death help avoid probate
- Annuities protect and immediately make proceeds available to the beneficiary
- There are no upfront sales charges allowing 100% of the money to be put to work for you, day one
- Most annuities have no fees (unless an optional rider is desired)

Though not the only goal, one of the main goals of annuities is to provide a steady stream of income during retirement. Funds accrue on a tax-deferred basis, and like 401(k) contributions, can only be withdrawn without penalty after age 59½.

Many aspects of an annuity can be tailored to the specific needs of the recipient. In addition to choosing between a single, lump sum payment or a series of payments to the insurer, you can choose when to begin taking income from your contributions. Remember, an annuity that begins paying out immediately is referred to as an immediate annuity, while those that start at a preset date in the future are called deferred annuities.

The duration of the payments, also called disbursements can also vary. You can choose to receive payments for a specific period of time; for example, a specified number of years or for your lifetime. Of course, securing a lifetime of payments lowers the amount of each check, but it helps ensure that you don't outlive your assets.

There are three main types of annuities; fixed, variable and fixed index annuities. One of the things that make annuities seem confusing is that the main street media and often Wall Street refer to all annuities without defining what type of annuity they are speaking. Therefore, the layperson can have a somewhat difficult time making sense of annuities, and what is said about them. If you thought that all cars were slow, you would not be able to understand how Ed Bolian, a 28-year-old from Atlanta, drove from New York City to Los Angeles, a 2,813-mile trip in 28 hours and 50 minutes. Once you know that all cars are not slow, and that he had a co-driver and an additional "support passenger," it can make sense, right?

Back to the annuity; likewise, if you blindly accepted an often-heard statement regarding annuities, "You cannot make any money with an annuity," you would not be able to comprehend how some annuity clients earned annual interest of more than 12% in 2013, or the 14 month review I recently did with a client that had an 18% return in 14 months. It is worth noting that this was without risk of their principal. These kinds of returns are not average or even frequent, but they do happen.

All three types of annuities are different, quite different in some cases. They each have their own level of risk and payout potential. Fixed annuities pay out a guaranteed amount based on the balance of your account. The downside of this predictability is a lower annual return, generally slightly higher to double that of a CD. You have the opportunity for a higher return, accompanied by greater risk, with a variable annuity. In this case, you pick from a menu of mutual funds that comprise your personal 'subaccount(s)'. Here, your payments in retirement are based on the performance of investments in your subaccount or it can have an optional income rider that provides a level of guarantees regarding income. Since your principal is invested in mutual funds, with a variable annuity, your principal is at risk.

Fixed index annuities, in my opinion, for many 55 and uppers are really the best of both annuity world extremes. Though the fixed annuity will typically keep pace with inflation better than CDs, the variable annuities are sold with talk of greater growth potential (keyword 'potential'), but without discussing the much greater risk involved. With the fixed index annuity, the owner can make money when the market goes up and not lose when the market goes down, and is therefore principal protected. There will be more on this later but, with a fixed index annuity, also known as an FIA, you receive a guaranteed minimum rate of return. But you have the potential to earn interest based on differing crediting strategies as well as different market indices, such as the S&P 500, which can earn significantly more.

It is the variable annuity that almost always has high fees. High fees, as well as risk, are inherent with the underlying subaccounts. Unfortunately for 55 and uppers, the media leads them to incorrectly think that all annuities have high fees, which is not the case. I am not certain whether these 'talking heads' don't know what they don't know, or if they are influenced by their advertisers, that have an interest in you not having a fixed, principal protected type of annuity. Why? Because it would mean you would have to take it out of their Wall Street 'game' and their financial advertisers are more often than not in the same game.

All cars are not created equal and neither are annuities. Any vehicle called a car of course has some things in common, but I think it is fair to say that a Lexus 460 and the ill-fated Yugo GV are not the same. All cars have four wheels (almost all, some have 3), an engine, transmission, a fuel system, a gas tank, a steering wheel, etcetera, right? Certainly no one vehicle serves the needs, wants and finances of every driver. Some people want a hybrid, some want the latest in technical design, some want a high-performance vehicle, and yet others want a car that is reliable, something solid, proven, with a good history. Additionally, not all drivers want to know exactly how every system inside the vehicle is designed. How the fuel is safely transported from the gas tank to the injectors or carburetor, how the combustion takes place and moves the pistons to turn the crankshaft to move the drive train to turn the wheels on so on, you get the point. Some drivers just want to know they can get in that the vehicle is going to very dependable, start up, go into gear, do what a well-designed vehicle is supposed to do, and get them safely to where they want to go. Likewise, I can say after assisting many 55 and uppers, not all annuity owners are the same either. Go figure.

Similarly, annuities have some things in common but the different types can be, and are very different. Like some car owners, some annuity buyers want to know, in detail, how all the parts of the annuity work together. They want to know exactly how every system inside the vehicle is designed. How the fuel (from different indices) (indexed crediting strategies) is safely transported from the gas tank (different indices) to the injectors (crediting strategies) or carburetor, they want to know how the combustion (bonus, tax deferral, guaranteed IAV growth) effect the movement of the pistons (cap rates and spreads) to turn the crankshaft to move their retirement (annuity) vehicle steadily and dependably in the direction they want to go.

But, just like other car owners, some annuity buyers just want to know that like their car, the annuity vehicle they purchase is going to start up the way they were told it would, and it will do what it was designed to do; get them, financially speaking, safely and dependably to where they want to go. Before we get into more specifics about each of the three types of annuities, let me first tell you what all three types of annuities have in common.

For all intents and purposes all annuities provide income tax deferral of the interest they earn. Therefore, annuities are said to have 'triple compounding.' They earn interest on your principal, the money you put in, interest on the interest that that is not withdrawn and interest on the money that would have otherwise had to be taken to pay taxes. Unlike a CD, where along with the little bit of interest you receive, you also get what? You get a 1099 and must withdraw money from somewhere, to pay the income taxes, meaning that you now lose the growth on that money. This is one of the reasons; once people understand this, many of them prefer a fixed (CD-like) annuity over a traditional CD. Just a note; the exception to the tax deferral of all annuities is when the annuity is owned by an entity instead of an individual or an annuity is being held in a trust for an individual.

Since all annuities are tax deferred, also known as tax qualified, the taxes are due and payable on a LIFO or last in, first out basis. That means that for example, you purchase/invest in an annuity with $100,000 and after 10 years of an average annual interest rate of 5% the annuity has grown to $162,889. You would have to pay income taxes on the growth of $62,889. Once you get down to the original $100,000 you put in to begin with, there would be no income tax due. That is, assuming the money you put in was after tax dollars, not a 401(k), IRA, etcetera. If the money that is put into an annuity is qualified retirement account money such as a 401(k) or IRA then Uncle Sam is going to get their (in my opinion, unfair) share on all the money, since no tax would have been paid on the money thus far. Am I the only one that finds it interesting that our loving, caring Uncle Sam made himself partners on the growth of our 401(k)? Huh!? That's right; they get a cut, a much bigger cut than they did when we used to have pensions. Am I the only one that thinks this is no coincidence?

Because of the "retirement nature and purpose" of annuities, they offer some protections from creditors in many states. One annuity may be exchanged for another annuity in accordance with the Internal Revenue Code Section 1035(e) without triggering a taxable event. These exchanges can be done at any time regardless of age of the owner or the annuitant.

All annuities are protected by various State Guaranty Funds. These reserve funds are maintained by each of the 50 states to safeguard and protect the cash value of annuity and life insurance contracts up to certain limits. These guaranty funds would come into play in the unlikely event that an issuing insurance company could not meet its obligations under the contract(s). You can review these state funds at www.nolgha.com .

Inherent in annuity contracts, there is a lot of flexibility and options for the payout phase. Owners can opt for a single lump sum payment upon maturity or one of various payment options for the remainder of life. It could be either over a single lifetime or even joint lifetimes in the case of married couples. There is also the option of taking 'periodic payments' usually no shorter than two years and no longer than thirty years. Another option owners like is a payout that is for a certain period, with a life option. That means if the annuitant dies before the payout period ends (for example 10 years), the payments would continue to be paid to the named beneficiary until the end of the contracted payout period.

In the next chapter, we will be talking more about *fixed index annuities* or FIAs, also sometimes called equity indexed annuities, but it is worth mentioning here that with FIAs there is even more flexibility as they have no set, or initially contracted payout schedule. This design is often favored by 55 and uppers because in retirement the owner can decide each year (or monthly or quarterly) how much he or she would like to withdraw, subject to the limitations and charges of the surrender charge period, like taking money from a savings account when you need or want it. As you will be reading shortly, FIAs also offer owners a guaranteed income for life option with a payment schedule provided by the insurance company. A very good thing is that with many fixed index annuities, this does not prevent the owner from having access to his or her remaining account balance.

A common feature of all annuities is the death benefit. The death benefit can vary though with some companies still applying the surrender penalties if still in force, and other companies waive any remaining surrender charges upon death. Before you make any annuity buying decisions be sure you know how the death benefits feature works. With FIAs typically the death benefits are paid in full upon the death of the annuitant without any surrender charges.

"Don't even think about getting an annuity. You will never be able to get your money out and if you do it will cost you a lot." "Did that agent tell you about the God-awful surrender penalties?" Those are just two of the often-given warnings, by whom I refer to as Wall Streeters, to keep potential annuity buyers from taking some of their money out of Wall Street. "Let's talk about that nasty, dirty, rotten, money grubbing, low down surrender charge;" another statement of misdirection. I am grateful they are there. At first, I did not understand it, how it works or why the insurance company came up with it. Once I understood the reasons the surrender charge is there and how it works, then I realized it is not the surrender penalty that is bad, it is the advisor that does not explain them.

You see, I am a FIA owner myself. I agreed to purchase a fixed index annuity with what I consider to be a long contract period. Contract periods usually range from 5 to 16 years. I own one that is a 14-year contract and therefore also has a 14-year surrender charge period. That means that I have contractually said to the insurance company that I will not take any of that money out in the 1st year and after the first year I will not take out more than 10% of the of the money I put in plus 10% of the growth. It does not mean I cannot take more than 10%, it just means I agreed to pay the required surrender charges on any amount over the allowable, agreed upon amount. In my case that is 10% of my principal and 10% of the growth, in the first year. Oh, also 10% of the upfront bonus I received when I put some of my retirement nest egg into the FIA. (More on that in a minute. I don't want to get things muddled up here). Typically, any surrender charge will decrease each year you own the annuity.

You see, part of the way the insurance companies' model works is related to long-term bonds and bond rates. They take a large portion of the money put into FIAs and they purchase long term, high quality bonds. They then take the guaranteed income received from these bonds and purchase options and this is one of the ways that insurance companies earn a reliable, solid profit. I want them to be profitable. What the heck, they are guaranteeing me future income. I want to know I can count on them to hold up their end. So here is the thing; they are depending on me holding up my end, including the terms of the contract. (I know, shocking, huh?) I am confident that I will too. On the other hand, maybe someone else who bought an annuity from the same company for whatever reason does not hold up their end and decides to take some or all their money out early. Well, now the insurance company must sell some of the long-term bonds to give them their money back early. That costs the insurance company money they did not plan on having to spend. This would affect their profit, if another party did not pay the costs. Remember,

I want the company to profit. So, the insurance company's options are to spread the cost of that annuity owner's decision not to abide by the agreement amongst all the annuity owners of which I am one, or to charge the annuity owner that reneged on the agreement. I like the fact that the party that did not abide by the agreement is the one paying, not me. I want my money in my annuity to continue to grow, tax deferred until I am ready to start taking some of it as income to live on. I do not want to pay for other people that make different, possibly less sound and unsure financial decisions.

Now, let me also say that none of us can know exactly what the future holds and unexpected things do happen. That is why it is very important to "never put more money into an annuity than you are confident you can leave in accordance with the surrender period." That is a 100% certain way of never incurring any surrender charges, ever. That does not mean it will never happen but I am very clear about that issue and want to err on the side of caution if there is any doubt.

Not only in regards to the surrender charges, but many things relating to the sale of annuities; something that is a concern to me is that not all annuity type advisors, telling the full truth and nothing but the truth any better than some of the Wall Streeters. Whether it is the surrender charges or something else, it cannot be overstated that it is ultimately important to be sure you are getting the whole story, clearly in a way you understand it. That way you can help your financial professional help you to make the absolute best decisions for your situation.

I do not mean to belabor this issue but there are some other things to know about surrender charges and the liquidity inherent in annuities. Most FIAs have what is called a "10% Free Withdrawal" after the first year. That being said, there are other more liquid options, including 100% liquidity, as well. Some of these options are recent developments and others have been around for a while. There is also something referred to as "cumulative free withdrawal." It might work like this. You may take 10% after the first year; if you do not take anything in year two you can take 20% in year three, and so on all the way up to 50% liquidity. There is another version of this which allows you to withdraw 20% surrender charge free;

in the beginning of contract year three, if you did not take anything in year two, and then this alternates until the end of the contract allowing you to take 20% in any year you took nothing the previous year. I know, this is getting confusing but stick with me here, as there is more.

There is something called a "return of premium" option offered on some annuities. While enough to satisfy most annuity needs, it is certainly, not on the majority of annuities. Depending on the company and the annuity, this can be a "no cost" option or in some cases there is a cost, known as a rider charge. What! Another charge? Yep. Just don't pay for it, don't buy it unless it makes sense. Easy enough. The "return of premium" works like this. You want your money (also called premium) back—all your money—so you exercise your return of premium option. They... return your premium, 100% less any withdrawals, fees or charges incurred, if any. For some annuity buyers, this gives them the peace of mind to know that just in case I need or want all my money back, I can get it. It is important to note that if you are several or more years into your annuity contract, it may be more advantageous to just surrender it instead of exercise the return of premium option. Here is why. Let's say you are hypothetically in year six of a ten year annuity contract. Your annuity account has grown by, let's hypothetically say, 14% and your surrender charge for year six is 7%. It makes more sense to pay the 7% and take the remainder of your growth, in this example 7%. Hope this is making sense.

There are many companies that now offer annuities. Some offer only a few while others offer many. If you decide that an annuity may possibly be right for protecting some of your retirement money just be sure to get an annuity that serves your specific purpose. That includes the liquidity issues. It would certainly not be a good idea, if you are 77 years old to put the majority of your money, or maybe even any of your money into a contract that was 16 years. On the other hand, typically it is the longer-term annuities that have better terms and with professional advice you will be able to find the right annuity to meet your specific needs.

Annuities are like an IRA in the sense that if you take your money out before you are 59 ½ you would be assessed a 10% penalty by the

Internal Revenue Service. There are numerous exceptions to that rule, and disability would be one example. There are distribution rules that relate to early withdrawal.

Let's talk for a minute about bonus premiums. Remember the days when the bank would give you a toaster for opening a savings account? Well, as part of the insurance company's' strategy to attract money, one of the things some of them do is offer a bonus.

Both agents and clients seem to love FIAs with bonuses. What is a bonus? It's simply when an insurance company takes the premium paid and bonuses that value for accumulation purposes. For example, if a client put $100,000 premium into a product with a 10 percent bonus, the account value for accumulation purposes start at $110,000 on day one.

The client sees it as a freebie and a way to increase the amount of money they have growing in the annuity. The bonus may be vested right away or it may vest over time. If it is vested right away, it would likely have a higher surrender charge than an annuity with a bonus that vests over time. Except in the situation of the death of the annuitant, in which case the premium and the bonus are usually paid out in full.

I am going to take a wild guess that you already know this, but nothing is free and that includes "free money" or annuity bonus money. In order to provide an up-front bonus, insurance companies must adjust the product so it remains profitable for them too. This is typically done by either extending the period, increasing the surrender charge amount, or by lowering the caps on the interest you can earn. Many annuity buyers like the upfront addition to their money. They like the growth to their principal (premium) put into the product and they like the growth on the bonus money too.

Now, having stated that, just know that the bonus does not serve every situation or every person; just like there is no one annuity that works best for all people. I will state again: It is important to know what the features of any annuity are that you are considering. Know how the features, charges, crediting methods and terms serve you, or not.

It is a hotly debated issue in the industry whether a big bonus FIA with a lower cap is better than a higher cap product with no bonus. We will talk more about caps in a bit. For now, you just need to know that the caps have a lot to do with what your annual interest or gain will be. As stated above, a company may lower the caps to pay the bonus. But it is impossible to say whether getting the additional growth on the bonus money from the first day of your contract will be better than no bonus with better cap rates. I have heard all sides but there is no definitive proof that one is always going to work better than the other. There are examples of both being better at different times, in different market conditions, with differing start dates. It would certainly be easy, after a football game is over to look back and say, if we had done this or that, we would have done better, scored more points. The same is true for fixed index annuities. Problem though, both with football and FIAs is that no one has a crystal ball. Well, more accurately, one that can be counted on.

One of the key features—really, what originally made an annuity an annuity is the ability to sometimes even the intention to annuitize the annuity. That means, you ask the insurance company to take the amount of money your annuity has grown into and to pay you an income stream. I touched on this earlier but what was not said is that 'annuitization' has one inherent and big drawback. Once you annuitize your money you have given it to the insurance company. It is now their money and in exchange, they pay you over the designated period you choose. Remember, like the pensions of the old days, when an employer would take the money put aside for your retirement, buy an annuity from an insurance company and annuitize it.

The downside is if you need a lump sum of money later there is no lump sum to be had. You chose payments. Another thing; let's say you have a half a million dollars in an annuity, you annuitize it, meaning you decide to take payments and you only live for a year. In many cases the insurance company keeps the money that did not get paid to you. There are some options and exceptions like a payout on two lives, your lifetime and the lifetime of your spouse. That means that the money would be paid out to the remaining spouse for the specified period, several years or the remainder of the spouse's life, depending on what payout you chose. This I do not prefer. I had a lady that came to see me and that is exactly what happened. Her husband retired from a defense company in Southern California and with poor or little advice opted for the pension annuity offered within his company plan upon retirement. He had just over $500,000 in his thrift savings plan and it was converted to a monthly income to be paid to him for the rest of his life. He died 6 months later and his spouse lost that income forever, at the same time she lost her husband of many years.

What option was there for this employee that would have not only provided him the lifetime of income he wanted and needed without the risk of losing his lump sum of money, or his account value? Answer: a fixed index annuity. That is the option. If he had transferred his money via an IRS qualified direct transfer to an IRA, outside of his company plan, he could have purchased a fixed index annuity, which does not work that way. You will learn in a minute that with a fixed index annuity and a guaranteed lifetime income rider, you are not required to annuitize the annuity to receive an income stream for life. You do not have to turn your bucket of money over to the insurance company for the income stream. To say that is a much better option is an understatement. Fifty-five and uppers really like this feature and you can certainly see why. It is always better to have more flexibility and options when it comes to your money. We can make a plan, a strategy that we anticipate will serve us best but sometimes life unfolds differently than we expect. When it does it is not just better to be able to get to a lump sum if needed, it is much better.

A common area ripe for misunderstanding and miscommunication is the conversation that many advisors have with pre-retirees and early retirees explaining the "dollars per month" the client will have to spend during retirement. Advisors tend to talk in terms of "income" planning, and they do this down to a monthly or annual amount. One thing that I have come to learn is that retirees tend to substitute the word "paycheck" for "income" in their own heads. Inevitably a chasm develops because the retiring employee having grown accustomed to a paycheck; a net paycheck (already reduced by taxes and benefit payments), throughout the last 50 years, and assumes 'income' means 'spendable.' It is important to understand how annuity income is taxed so there are no surprises.

Annuity income can be generated with qualified money. Money, you have not yet paid tax on like IRA, 401(k), 403(b) etcetera. If you have not paid income tax, you will when it comes out as income. Income from annuities can also be generated from money you have paid tax on. In this case the taxation of the payments falls under Section 72 of the IRS code. This section details the mechanics and tax treatment of each annuitization payment—known as the exclusion ratio. In essence, the exclusion ratio treats each annuity payment as a "slice" of the bigger pie. In other words, each annuity payment is deemed to have a proportionate amount of basis and interest growth—thus spreading the taxes over time. In tax parlance, this is known as a tax preference.

The exclusion ratio described within the IRS code is best understood as a simple fraction applied to each monthly or annual annuity payment. The numerator is the amount of after tax money, or what's known as "basis," within the annuity. Since that money has already been taxed, it's excluded from taxation, as it is annuitized. Let's look at an example where a retiree puts $100,000.00 of after tax money into an annuity and it is annuitized using a 10-year certain annuitization option which pays out $1,500.00 per month for 120 months. You will see in this example the exclusion amount (non-taxable portion of the annuity payment) is determined by dividing basis (or amount you put in) by the total "expected return" through annuitizing and then multiplying that by the amount of the monthly annuity payment.

As an example, if $100,000.00 of after tax money was put into an annuity, the expected total return (or total amount of payments) is $180,000. The percentage derived by the division, in this case is .555, that is multiplied by $1500.00 (the monthly payment). That would get you to a dollar amount of $833.33, which would be the amount, excluded from taxation. Carrying this out to spendable income looks like this (assuming a 25 percent federal/state combined rate). Monthly income $1500.00, less the excluded (from income tax) amount of $833.33 = taxable income of $666.67. Now assuming a combined 25% tax rate would mean $166.67 is the income tax due. So, $1500.00 less the income tax of $166.67 means that the 'spendable dollars' from the annuitization are $1,333.33.

If you are a 55 and upper, thinking that an annuity is worth considering for some part of your retirement income, please know it is very important when you are talking with an annuity advisor, that they speak "your language" not their industry language. This will help to prevent any ugly surprises, like being short of monthly income to live on. I have found that my main job, the most important thing I can do for 55 and uppers, is to communicate in a way that allows them to 'really' see their situation clearly, maybe for the first time. Then, (they) can be a huge part of putting together a strategy that is not only theirs alone but more importantly, one that will work for their unique, individual situation.

Here is an example of what can happen when potential annuity buyers correctly understand the way it works. It is not uncommon for a conversation (where there is real understanding) to lead to a decision to extend the payout period and reduce the amount taken out every month due to the tax preference that accrues to the client through the exclusion ratio. Or if the client needed the full $1,500 every month, they could make some adjustments to expenses or alternatively, take a shorter annuitization schedule.

Keep in mind, we have only looked at one annuity payout option, and there are many. Remember, with a fixed index annuity, you can still have growth added to your annuity account. Even though you may have initiated your annuity with money you have already paid the tax on any growth will still be subject capital gains taxation.

Withdrawal-based income

Not all annuity owners annuitize their annuity for income. There are two other ways income can be and often is structured. The annuity owner can take income payments using "free" withdrawals allowable under the contract and/or by exercising their income rider if they opted for that. By choosing to take income from free withdrawals or the income rider, you do not turn your lump sum over to the insurance company in exchange for the annuity payments. For this reason, the account value is left in place to continue to grow through additional interest credits.

Now here's where things can get a little complicated—withdrawals taken and payments made under the income rider are not treated the same as payments resulting from annuitization. Remember from earlier, withdrawals are considered interest first, followed by basis. So, to the extent there are gains, including any bonus given and growth, those dollars will be deemed to come out first, before principal or basis. As a result, the income coming out of the annuity early on (when income begins) will be subject to income tax until all the growth has come out. At that point withdrawals would be coming out of your basis and therefore not taxable. Again, this taxation method is referred to as LIFO. In this example, the last money in (interest or growth) is considered paid out first and therefore taxable.

As an example, assume $100,000 of after tax money was put into a 10 percent premium bonus annuity. The plan is to leave it alone for the first year and use the 10 percent free withdrawal provision to provide $10,000 of income during the second year. This will give the annuity time to accrue interest credits. Starting in the third year, scheduled income withdrawals will begin. Even if we assume no interest credits to the account, the account value starting day one of the second year is $110,000 because of the bonus. Since withdrawals are deemed to be earnings first, basis later, the entire $10,000 ($833 per month) free withdrawal is taxable. For someone needing a monthly paycheck of $833, but instead receives only $625, that could come as quite a shock ($10,000/12 compared to $7,500/12). Now, do you see why it is so important to be absolutely certain you are speaking with, working with a financial professional that tells you the whole story? No one wants an ugly surprise like that. If this kind of tax treatment is not communicated and planned for, such an unforeseen event could cause a lot of upset, or worse.

When someone decides to protect some of their hard-earned money with a fixed index annuity, they will need to move their money from where it is now, and inform their risk advisor to move it from the protected 'green' basket. Your current advisor does not want you to move your money! Please be prepared to hear things like, "The only reason that so and so annuity agent/advisor is selling you that, no good, useless, dirty, lowdown annuity is because of the unbelievably high commission that he/she is earning." This is one of the things often stated by Wall Street advisors that do not want to lose any portion of your assets to another advisor or financial professional. As is most often the case, this is a half-truth. As I have said before, half-truths are, in my opinion much more dangerous and devious than full out lies. Why? Because they are plausible, they are believable. So... let's clarify another thing.

Are annuity commissions high? Well, as in all cases, I think the individual should be allowed to decide for himself or herself, once given the whole truth. I have great faith in people to make decisions that are good for them if they have sufficient information—both sides. Annuity commissions vary from under 2% to some annuities that pay 8%, and on rare occasion even higher. The commission is determined by many factors, including crediting strategies, the type of annuity (variable, fixed, fixed index, etc.) but the main determinant is the contract term. Let's take the example of a fixed index annuity with a 14-year contract. That annuity will pay a larger commission than a 5-year fixed rate annuity. Why? Because if you have a financial professional, one truly getting paid because they are looking out for you vs. selling you 'something', one that has your best interest at heart, that person will be your advisor; your financial professional for 14 years. He or she is being paid to work for you for 14 years! There are several popular 14-year annuities with a 10% bonus premium. These pay on average a 7% commission. If you do the math that is one half a percent commission for each year of advice.

Just like, not all Wall Street advisors have your best interest at heart when they tell you "The only reason that agent/advisor is selling you that, no good, useless, dirty, lowdown annuity is because of the unbelievably high commission that he/she is earning," not all annuity advisors have your best interest at heart either. What! There are self-centered annuity advisors too? Yes! I will tell you that if you were to opt for a 14-year annuity, your advisor got paid a 7% commission and then you did not hear from them, they did not provide you 14 years' worth of valuable advice, and service, that is...a very high commission.

Now, here is something interesting. The same Wall Streeters that are telling you not to pay one half percent commission per year are on average charging double, triple that or more, in one or multiple ways. I refer to that as a "look over there." While they have you looking 'over there' where the annuity advisor is earning ½ percent (in this example) per year commission, you will not be able to 'look over here,' where you are very likely paying out much more than ½ percent per year with them.

Also in regards to high commissions paid for annuities it is important to know that the money paid to annuity advisors does not come directly out of the buyer's money. The commission is paid out as part of the insurance company's expenses. Now that being said, if the agent did not need to be paid, in other words if they would work for nothing like so many other people (lol), your return or growth on the annuity would likely be more, yes. But, those darned advisors have families that want to eat too. So, the point of this is that if, in the example above, one purchased a 14-year annuity with $100,000.00 and opted for a 10% bonus, the account value of their annuity would be $110,000.00 on the very first day of their contract. With typical death benefit features these days, if the annuitant were to die that evening the beneficiary would receive the $110,000.00. Or, another way to put it is that when you put money into an annuity 100% of your money goes to work in the annuity. There are no commissions that come out of your money. Alright, so that is what there is about commissions.

Another thing that many people have heard is, "the fees are high!" If that statement is being made about a variable annuity, it would be correct. If it is being made about a fixed or fixed index annuity it would not be true. The problem here is that these kinds of statements are made all the time without clarification, another murky 'look over there'; if you will. Look over there, at that annuity (which one, fixed or variable, hmmm?), the fees are high. Don't look over here where we are charging you, quite likely much more. I do not know whether it is the case that the media, the TV talking heads and Wall Streeters just don't know what they don't know or if they actually do understand the 'true' annuity story and don't want it to get out. Let's talk about the types of annuities a bit more.

Annuities...what's your type?

Let's start with "the fees are high" type of annuity, variable annuities. A **variable annuity** is a tax-deferred vehicle that allows you to choose from a selection of investments via "sub-accounts." They can provide income determined by the performance of the underlying investments you choose or in some cases provide minimum guaranteed income via an income rider. Like mutual funds, variable annuities carry the risk of loss of principal. Variable annuities provide life insurance, typically equal to your original deposit. This allows advisors selling variable annuities to say something like, "Don't worry you will always be able to at least get back what you put in." Unfortunately, they do not clearly communicate that you must die first. No small detail!

Like any market investment, variable annuities (VA) are time sensitive and subject to market risk. However, unlike other investments and safe money products, variable annuities don't seem to recover well at all when they lose. Even today many retirees and investors haven't recovered losses in VA products to the levels they were in 2007. Many investment professionals often criticize variable annuity contracts, which are saddled with very high fees; rightfully so, in my opinion. Just remember anytime you hear, "annuity fees are high," with 99 percent certainty, it is the variable annuity they are referring to, even if they do not say that. With typically expensive rider fees on top of the other typical, average annual fees of up to 2.7%, the average total charges are 3.7%. That is an average. Some are higher. To say they are criticized for being expensive is an understatement. Compare that to the fact that ninety nine percent of fixed index annuities have no fees. Now, here is an OOTTTMYSH for you. (One Of Those Things That Make You Say Hmm). The same advisors that tell you not to buy a fixed index annuity by leading you to believe that fees are high for all annuities (by telling a half-truth) are the only ones selling variable annuities, which actually have the high—the very high fees. If that isn't an OOTTTMYSH, nothing is.

Besides being expensive, variables are thought by many professionals to be ineffective complicated sub accounts; mutual funds not nimble enough to navigate the challenging market times we now live in. Add to this the deadly pro rata system, which is used to calculate guaranteed income and the death benefits, and sadly some clients can become trapped in products that underperform. In horse racing terms, it wouldn't be out of order to say variable annuities aren't good 'come from behind' runners, and once they lose their position they seldom regain it. It is precisely factors like these that make it critical to evaluate any variable annuity contract you may have or are considering for the future. Like all investments, there comes a time to hold them and definite reasons to fold them! In this mode, you may lose precious principal and deplete the death benefit you eventually intended to leave to your love ones.

One issue with variable annuities is timing. If you owned a variable annuity contract in 1999, you were likely pleased at your prior year's performance, even though many variable contracts underperformed most mutual funds during this time. Twelve years later, however, the story was much different. Many of these same variable contracts were floundering below their 1999 levels. They had endured a crippling loss and never regained it all. Meanwhile, the regular market indexes and safer vehicles climbed back above their 1999 levels. Even more problematic, many variable annuity owners who took income from these products while the markets were tanking saw their principal drop to insignificant levels, and they couldn't take advantage when the bull market began anew. There were thousands of complaints to the SEC filed against variable products.

In response to falling sales, and the market debacle of 2000-2002, the variable annuity industry added so called, "guarantee features." These guarantees, assured contract holders that they would be able to take certain percentage of the amount they had originally put into the contracts yearly. Usually, this was for life, regardless of a declining overall balance in your account. There is also the aforementioned death and the annuitization option with minimum guarantees. But remember you are giving up your money at this point. You'll never see any more growth. You will never get your principal back. But is this a good deal? Most say no way, and the guarantee wears thin when compared to real guarantees of no loss of principal (ever) and getting your money back in a lump sum.

But again, to be fair, everyone should make their own decisions.

For instance, if a policyholder purchased his or her contract in the midst of a strong bull market then it would appear these contracts can do well. If, however they are purchased at the beginning of a bear market, or, during their ownership they entered a severe bear market, the performance of a typical variable annuity frequently becomes paltry and stagnant. As one ex-variable annuity insurance executive with Pacific Life, Jacob Dinan stated, "The insurance companies are just not set up to manage their variable annuity portfolios to the extent really needed when things turn sour or go flat... that's why they were crushed in 2000 and again in 2008." This is why a variable annuity does not belong in the green bucket of 'Know So' money. That is why it is not the best choice for most retirees. It is more 'Hope So' money. Expensive and typically, little managed Hope So money.

Significant market drops have put some variable companies under great duress and to compensate, some have increased fees by charging the maximum amount allowed by contract. Likewise, they raised the fees on new contracts and lowered the percentage you could take out per year on the guaranteed income side. The problem with the pro rata calculation is that over time, the principal death benefit and guaranteed income balances can erode more quickly. They can even fall to the point that neither the contract holders nor their heirs can get a substantial lump sum from the contract. More insidious is that contract holders may eventually be forced to annuitize the contract, forfeiting all control and all the potential earning power of their monies. For the above reasons, I believe variable annuities are not optimum market vehicles for growth or the best option for principal protection and income, which is what retirees want and need.

I think a far better strategy, is to keep things separate, simple, and clean. In my view the average retiree is much smarter if they focus on certainty, for the money they are counting on living on. That generalized strategy, professionally designed for your individual needs and retirement goals, has a significantly better chance to secure your retirement, no matter what. It is 'Know So' money versus 'Hope So' money. If after providing sufficient guaranteed income to give you peace of mind, you can take more risk with the remaining money you are not counting on needing in the near term, say 1-10 years. You can be more aggressive using actively managed portfolios that offer everything from dividend, paying stocks to bond portfolios to exchange traded funds. Overall, this is a safer, less confusing, and more flexible approach that avoids the variable annuity's main dilemma; they only do well in the best of times. In summary, it is wise to always remember that variable annuities are in many ways, fair-weather products whose benefits tend to disappear very quickly in declining, flat or mediocre markets.

For the variable annuity, one must consider the issues of timing, a track record of limited performance, high fees, pro-rata deductions and the market devastations of 2000 and 2007. All this history makes it critical that anyone in one of these contracts now should assess them thoroughly and be ready to adjust and change accordingly, if they can. If they don't, they might as well stop calling their contracts variable annuities and substitute the phrase 'Voluntary Annuitization Vehicles.' Why? Because that's what's happening, people are turning over their principal and all the lifetime earning power of their money by annuitizing. Something no one would l likely choose at the outset. Remember, if you want your principal to vary, go up and go down when you least expect it and maybe can least afford it, a variable is one way to do that.

On the other hand

On the other hand if you do not want your principal to vary, you want it to always be there when you need it, then you must know more about the **fixed annuity.** It is a contract with an insurance company. One of the contractually guaranteed benefits is that your principal is protected against loss. Fixed annuities may be either single premium or flexible premium. Single premium means you put all the money in, one time, at the beginning of the contract. A flexible premium fixed annuity allows you to put additional monies in after the initial purchase.

With a **'deferred' fixed annuity,** you receive a guaranteed amount of interest which accumulates inside of the annuity contract.

The interest is tax deferred, so no income taxes are paid until you take a withdrawal. A deferred fixed annuity typically has surrender charges that are in place for a period of anywhere from 3 to 10, or more years. Most deferred fixed annuities have a feature that allows you to access up to 10% of the contract value each year without having to pay any surrender charge. Some allow for 100% return of your premium at any time also. Be sure to consider your liquidity needs before deciding.

With an **'immediate' fixed annuity,** you exchange your lump sum of money for a guaranteed stream of income from the insurance company. Once fixed annuity payments begin, they do not change, which means they will not increase with inflation, unless of course you opt for a payout that provides some version of increase, for example; cost of living or fixed annual increase, say 2% of income. A single premium immediate annuity, also known as a SPIA begins paying you income immediately. There is no accumulation or growth phase. It is simply, here insurance company is "X" amount of dollars, how much will you pay me in equal payments for "X" number of years.

Keep in mind, once these annuity payments begin, you no longer own, or have access to, the principal. You simply have a right to the income they have promised you. You have annuitized. Once you choose to annuitize your contract, which means you trade in your lump sum for a guaranteed stream of income, you must choose the term of your payments. When considering a fixed annuity, you should also look at the fixed index annuity as an option. It allows for withdrawals as well as income payout without having to turn over your principal to the insurance company. Therefore, your bucket of money has the potential to continue to grow even while receiving income. Also, if done properly, you will still have access to any lump sum balance, subject to any remaining surrender charge, if applicable.

A TSA. There is a special class of annuities governed by Section 403(b), 457 and other Internal Revenue Code; a TSA or **tax sheltered annuity.** They can be fixed or variable. These annuities are generally available to public employees, teachers, police officers, those that work for non-profits, and some private sector employees that work under government contract. Like a 401(k), the money going into these annuities is pre-tax and therefore taxable later as ordinary income. Premiums are usually made via regular payroll deductions, like a 401(k). The contribution and withdrawal options vary widely, sometimes even depending on the individual circumstances of the owner. One caveat if you own a TSA; be careful annuitizing (handing over your money to the insurance company in exchange for income) when you retire. You do not want to be the person that converts a large sum of money into payments, passes away early leaving nothing for loved ones. An option would be to do a properly structured, tax qualified, 'direct transfer' instead, and then get an annuity; a fixed index annuity with your TSA lump sum. Remember, you can take income and/or withdrawals without giving up your account value with a fixed index annuity.

Prior to 2010, the best-selling fixed index annuity in America had been a payout **two-tier annuity** requiring clients to withdraw their money in installments. It is exactly that 'requiring' that limits their flexibility and therefore not suitable for too many people. Flexibility is always better. Their popularity has decreased significantly with the new, considerably more effective products for accomplishing what most annuity buyers want; principal protection with upside potential and flexibility. This also means these newer designs are suitable for a lot more fifty-five and uppers.

So why were they so popular? Because the marketing is principally focused on the higher tier while the explanation of the lower tier is typically far less explained. A "look over there." Look over there where you see those great benefits, not over here where we don't want you to see the potential risks and limitations. Again remember, not all annuity advisors are created equal. Every type of annuity is suitable for some people but not every person is suited for some type of annuity. Let me repeat, every type of annuity is suitable for some people but not every person is suited for some type of annuity. Be aware of annuity sales people (in my opinion, they are not advisors, they are sales people) that do not explain or give the whole story. Sales people sell for commissions, a 'true' advisor advises, they educate and are compensated for their expertise, application of their knowledge and improving lives of others. Another reminder, half the story and half-truths, the 'look over theres', whether about stocks, bonds and mutual funds or about annuities can be insidious and wreak havoc on your retirement future.

With many two-tier annuities, earnings are reported as if clients will hold the annuity until the end of the contract term and then withdraw their money in installment payments over a certain number of years. If they don't take it in installment payments, earnings are computed in a very unfavorable fashion. With the typical payout two-tier, clients must withdraw their money over a period of at least 10 years to get the full account value reported on their annual annuity statement. Beneficiaries are generally permitted after the owner's death to obtain the full account value only if they withdraw the money in installments over five years. Should the owner or beneficiaries ever withdraw the money as a lump sum, a much lower rate of interest than the index-linked rate is paid for the entire life of the annuity—going all the way back to the date the account was opened. What's more, any bonus added to the account, and interest it has earned, will be taken back if a lump sum withdrawal is made.

There is no guarantee with payout two-tier annuities that the client's money will earn a rate of return during the installment payout period, typically a period of five to 10 years. With the payout two-tier annuity, they'll receive the interest credited during the accumulation period and the bonus added to the account only if they withdraw in installments. When the installment payments start, clients may receive a below-market rate of interest because the insurer is not obligated to pay a competitive interest rate.

On the other hand, if clients withdraw funds in a lump sum from a payout two-tier annuity they earn a much lower rate for the entire time they held the annuity and lose any bonuses received when they opened the account. Either way, they're likely to get smaller earnings from their money.

Chapter 9
Takeaways

- Retirees must understand that retirement is the 'spending' years. It is all about income and how to have enough for the rest of your life. The focus should be on a strong, dependable foundation of money you can depend on.
- Most financial advisors do not truly know how to plan income certainty. Their knowledge of annuity, pension-like income is very limited. Main reason; they sell risk oriented investments and strategies.
- Annuities can be a great, additional source of guaranteed income alongside social security. They need to be understood to make sure it is right for you, and that you are getting the one that serves your purpose most effectively.
- One reason annuities need consideration for retirees is because no other retirement investment vehicle provides longevity credits. It is an investment strategy, and tool for (living) longevity.
- Variable annuities do not protect your principal; something that should be important to someone that is no longer working.
- When it comes to money you will need to live on for the rest of your life, do you want to 'know' or is 'hoping' enough? Have the courage to follow your own path.

"Come to the edge," he said.
"We can't, we're afraid!" they responded.
"Come to the edge," he said.
"We can't, we will fall!" they responded.
"Come to the edge," he said.
And so they came.
And he pushed them.
And they flew."

—Guillaume Apollinaire—

Chapter 10

Knowing vs. Hoping

Retirement... the earning years are over. You are now in the spending years. The earning years were about getting here, about saving for right now. Asset-wise, financially speaking you have what you have. Figuring out the best way to get the most out of what you have is the retirement planning challenge. How to make what you have last as long as you. How to get the most living out of the money we have. We are in the last quarter of the game and we must play it right if we are to have peace of mind, longevity, and security. Building on the Rule of 100, we need to organize the types of investments and assets you have into a helpful visual. As they say, a picture is worth a thousand words. That is good because it is 4:30AM and I want to finish this chapter before I go to bed.

So, I am going to assign colors to the different kinds of money and their level of risk. For our purposes, the 'Know So' money, the safer and more dependable money is green. 'Hope So' money, the money that is exposed to risk and fluctuates with the market is red. Understanding this simple exercise is the key to having enough money to last for the rest of your lifetime. This is quite important! Possibly the most important lesson in this book. Everything has been leading up to this. There are numerous financial decisions to be made over the next 25 years. They all hinge on your asset allocation, deciding how much risk is too much.

Most fifty-five and uppers, retirees and soon to retirees don't know the level of risk they are exposed to. Allow me to digress a moment. I ask you to look at the graph below which shows that if you lose 50%, you need 100% gain just to get even. Warren Buffet said the first rule of investing is, "Never lose money." He said the second rule is, "Never forget the first rule."

The impact of losing is a BIG deal, particularly in retirement, for two reasons: 1) We do not have the same time horizon to get our money back and, 2) We are likely to need it and be forced to spend some when it is down; a big no-no in retirement. Look at the notes in the graph showing some of the drops we have had. We have had 50% drops and will have them again. John Bogle, founder of Vanguard was on CNBC Halftime report in April 2013 and said, we are going to have two drops of as much as 50% in the next 10 years. That is not hard to believe if you look at this graph. Another thing to consider, after almost 6 years of one of the biggest run-ups in the market we have ever seen, most people have just gotten the money back that they had in 2007. And they 'think' they are doing great because that is what the TV talking heads and media tell them. I have challenged every student, every client that tells me in one way or another that they have done great in the market, earning 7, 8, 9, 10 percent and more to prove that kind of growth over any extended period. I would even like to see it proven to me that someone has even earned an average 'real' rate of return of 5%. The indicators are borne out by the annual Dalbar report, most people after fees have taken all that risk just to barely keep up with inflation. So far no one has even attempted to prove they have earned even 5%. Looking at this snippet from the Dalbar report; it shows even though what we were sold was, 8, 9, 10, 11 percent and even higher returns, over a 30-year period ending in 2014, the average investor earned 3.69% annually. That is right. The S&P index averaged 11.11% for 30 years. The average investor got 3.69% according to Dalbar. Now subtract from that fees and/or costs. REALLY!? If they had told you, put a half a million dollars of your hard-earned money into a 401(k), and be willing to see losses of 50% sometimes and you will earn 3.69% less any fees or cost, would you have done it? I am guessing, not!

OK, back to the color of our money, green and red. How much of each? Organizing your assets so that you can 'see' them—visualizing them is an important and powerful way to get a clear picture of what kind of money you have, protected or risk. Know So or Hope So. It helps to see where it is and how you can make the most of it for retirement. This exercise is easy. Easy once you understand what is green and what is red, that is. It is just a matter of listing all your assets and assigning them a color based on their status as 'Know So' or 'Hope So' money. You may want to or need to work with a financial professional to create a comprehensive inventory of your assets as you categorize them. Be careful here. Not all or even very many financial professionals really understand 'true' asset diversification, or the 'Hope So' money vs. 'Know So' money. Most are thinking in terms of stock, bond and other risk type investments only or Wall Street only type of financial vehicles. It is all they know or maybe best put, all they sell. When that is the case, you will never have any money allocated to the green basket. The green basket is the protected, safer basket—the non-Wall Street category. It is very important to know where you are and to understand what you are working with before you make decisions that set the foundation for a plan that must serve you the rest of your life. This will very likely be the first time you have ever sat down and looked at all your assets in this manner. It will allow you to see how much money you have in the market, subject to risk of loss. Looking at the color of your investments will let you see where you are relative to the Rule of 100. For many it is a real eye opener.

Most people 'think' they are diversified. That is because that is what they have been told. To help you envision and better understand 'true' diversification versus what I have heard referred to as 'pixie dust' diversification I want to share a childhood story. I think it will help. Early in the book, I told you I was one of five boys. On Easter, we each got to color one dozen eggs. There were never two eggs alike. They were all different. They were DIVERESIFIED. One year we put all five-dozen colored eggs in a basket on the dining table in some of that fake green grass. We went to church and came home to find that our dog had gotten up on the table, knocked the basket off the table, and played with and even ate some of the eggs. There were not many eggs salvaged that could be used for our deviled eggs. ☹

So what does that have to do with anything you wonder? Well, think of this; if we had put some of those eggs in a different basket, put that basket in the cupboard or up on the refrigerator, those 'protected' eggs would have still been available for our use.

So, just as with our Easter eggs in 1965, you most likely have all your nest egg assets in one basket right now; the red basket. The risk basket. Those nest egg assets may be quite diversified as ours were, but... they are precariously, all in the same basket. When that basket was knocked off the table in 2008, it was devastating to all too many hopeful retirees and people "hoping" to be able to retire.

During your working years, it is likely that you have accumulated different types of assets. Assets can be money that you have in a savings, retirement accounts (401(k), 403b, IRA), rental income, home equity, Social Security, inheritance and pension as examples. There are others as well. You have likely worked hard and exercised some discipline to have this money. You have made financial decisions based on the best information you had at the time or, in reality for many... based on the 'lack of' real information. That was then this is now, what do we do with what we have? As we have seen, it's more important than ever to know how much of your assets are at risk. How many of the eggs you are counting on that are in the same basket? High market volatility and low savings rates can make it difficult to allocate money to keep up with inflation and offer protection at the same time. Properly allocating your nest egg assets, relative to risk is the foundation of asset management for the retirement years. Part of that consideration is taking into account your specific situation, the amount of assets you have, the life you want (hope) to live, your individual needs, how much certainty you want, etcetera.

Even though you 'feel,' even though you 'think' you have plenty of money in your 401(k) or IRA, not really understanding how much risk you are exposed to and how that risk is different when you are no longer working, can cause you major financial suffering. Just ask some of the retirees that lost half of their nest egg assets in 2008. Some of them had to sell and move to a less expensive area. Some had to go back to work (at low paying jobs), move in with relatives or have relatives move in with them. I could go on but you get the picture. If they had understood that having all their assets in the red (risk) basket was likely not a good idea as they neared retirement, they would have lost a lot less money going into retirement... and life would have been different, would be different today! Think about the Rule of 100. Subtract your age from 100. The remainder is the percentage limit of how much you should have in the red, risk basket. Remember, it is a rule of thumb. It is your money. You have worked for it, saved it. It is your life that will either flourish or flounder based on your asset allocation decisions. At the end of the day, if you are still comfortable with all your eggs in the red, risk basket, that is what you should do.

When using the Rule of 100 to calculate your level of risk, your financial age might be different than your real age, however. The way you allocate your assets also depends on your individual situation. Whatever you determine to be the right amount of risk is for you, you will need to organize your nest egg assets to reflect your goals and financial desires. If you have more Red Money than you desire, you will need to make decisions about what to do, how and where to move it so that it better suits you, so that it is more in line with the new information you are getting, your new reality... being retired, no more work ☺. You can and should work with a financial professional to find and better understand Green Money options for your situation.

The next step is to figure out the right amount and ratio of Green and Red Money. Investing heavily in Red Money and risking (gambling) all your assets on the market is incredibly precarious no matter where you fall, within the Rule of 100. It is risky to depend on money in the market to generate income, and a plan that leans too heavily on Red Money can easily fail, especially when investment decisions are influenced by your emotional reactions, or your advisors' reactions and guesses related to market downturns and recoveries. Timing the market has never been done successfully by anyone with consistency. It may be even more impacted by your advisors need to keep (all) your money in the red basket, so they can make the maximize their income, not yours. Not only is this an unwise plan, it can be incredibly stressful to an investor who is gambling everything on stocks, bonds, mutual funds and the many other pseudo 'alternative' red basket investments we were told would protect us in 2008. The issue, no matter how different your red basket investments are, is that they are still all in the red basket.

On the other hand, it is not wise to have all your assets in Green Money either. It is still important to leverage the potential for growth with some of your assets. You would not be diversified if all your assets were in the green bucket. Another thing, investing all your money in Certificates of Deposit (CDs), savings accounts, money markets and other low return accounts that likely won't keep pace with inflation is an insidious and silent retirement killer. You don't see the loss (of your spending power) on any statement. But, you are going broke slowly with each passing year.

Green Money becomes much more important in your fifties, sixties and beyond. Green Money can do something that Red Money can never do. It can provide (guaranteed) income. That is another reason Green Money investing and saving has grown by leaps and bounds as baby boomers retire in record numbers. It is a way for them to create their own pension-like additional income with some of their retirement money. As we near and enter retirement, you want to reduce the amount of Red Money you have and transition it to Green Money, but you don't necessarily need all of it to generate income for you right away or maybe ever. There are different types of Green Money. Some designed for great income; others are designed best as growth opportunity, while simultaneously protecting your principal.

We may have money we want to protect in the Green Money category that we need to spend now, need to spend later, or possibly never need to spend. Retirement planning for most people and for most intents and purposes is 'income' planning, or should be. It is about converting what you have into income when you need it in the most effective way possible, and hopefully in a way that you know not hope it is going to be there.

Money that you need to depend on must be in Green Money vehicles. There are two types of Green Money: Money used for income you need now and money used for accumulation to meet your income needs down the road in five, 10 or 20 years. Money needed for income now is money you need to meet your basic needs, to pay your bills, your mortgage if you have one and the costs associated with maintaining your lifestyle. Green Money used for accumulation is money that you don't need now for income, but will need to rely on down the road. It's still Green Money because you will rely on it later for income and will need to count on it being there; this money represents income your assets will need to generate for future use. When planning your retirement, it is vital to decide how much of your assets to structure for current income (if needed) and how much to allocate for accumulation to create income or legacy later. Yes, many people think of Green Money as leave behind money too because they know how much they are leaving.

So how do we optimize risk and find the right balance? Determining the amount of risk that is right for you depends on your specific situation. It starts by examining your individual and specific financial situation. Again, the Rule of 100 is a useful way to begin to determine the right amount of risk for you. But remember, it's just a place to start. Use it as a starting point for figuring out where your money should be. If you're a 50-year-old investor, the Rule of 100 suggests that you have 50 percent Green Money and 50 percent Red Money. Of course, 50-year-olds can afford to be more risk tolerant. There are several reasons why someone might decide to take more risk than indicated by the Rule of 100. Experienced investors may decide to gamble for a shot at higher returns, or sometimes people decide they need to gamble for a higher return (actually a scary strategy, if you know what I mean), or people who have met, or guaranteed their desired minimum retirement income goals may be looking for ways to accumulate more wealth. Again, it comes down to your personal tolerance for risk and maybe just as or even more importantly, the ability of your nest egg to take the hits and survive. What do I mean? I mean the more you have, the more you can afford to lose and still be OK, plain and simple.

Having an educated discussion with your financial professional is often the wisest approach to determining the risk level that is right for you. This assumes you have a financial professional that understands red versus green money. If their idea of diversification is limited to only stocks, bonds and mutual funds, red basket only, then it is a non-starter and you will need to find someone else. If that is your case, then you must make the effort necessary to find a professional that can, and is willing to make the time to help you determine your risk tolerance by getting to know you, asking you the right questions and doing the necessary homework to have back and forth discussion(s) needed to determine your comfort level with different types of risk as well as the ability of your nest egg to withstand risk. An example of some questions a financial professional might pose to you would be along these lines. You have $500,000 in your 401(k) and are retiring soon. There is an investment product that could turn your $500,000 into $600,000 or more. That same investment option, however, can turn your $500,000 into $350,000 or less. Is that a scenario you are comfortable with? Or would you feel better about a scenario where you could turn your $500,000 into $550,000, with no risk of loss?

Your answer to these types of questions and other types of questions will help you and the financial professional determine what level of risk is right for you. They should also be able to recommend asset allocation and investment strategies that reflect your financial age and particular situation.

Numbers don't lie; they are what they are. We have what we have and we need what we need. Though the decisions that need to be made can seem complicated but in reality, the numbers, your numbers, your specifics, how much you have, how much you spend, how long you are likely to live; these things will dictate your options. Your risk tolerance is an important indicator of what kinds of investments you should have in retirement, but if the returns from those investments don't meet or fit with your income goals then there will be problems. Possibly a problem you will not ever comeback from. Some professionals may encourage you to be more aggressive with your investment strategy by taking on more risk to give you the potential of earning a greater return. Of course, you know this is a double-edged sword. If taking more risk isn't an option that you are comfortable with, then sometimes the discussion needs to turn to either how you can earn (work for) more money and/or spend less so that you can align your needs with your resources, thereby providing what you need, as well as peace of mind.

How are you going to structure the flow of your income in retirement? This is a big part of the planning process. Not just income for the day you retire but income for 5, 10, 20, and for some even 30 years down the line. That plan, those decisions must include inflation, lifestyle desired, healthcare cost, death of spouse, legacy, required minimum distributions (RMDs), a decrease possibly in Social Security, as well as other uncertainties, some of which are unforeseeable. A frank and educated discussion and the answers to these questions and issues will have much to do with how you and your advisor determine your risk tolerance. Again, the numbers don't lie. You have to eat the elephant one bite at a time as they say, decision by decision. For example, if the numbers tell you that you have insufficient assets to provide the income you need to pay for the lifestyle you want, for the time you anticipate living, then it becomes a choice, a decision. You can take greater risk with your assets, work longer and/or save more. Though many advisors would, (I think you know) I would not recommend taking greater risk. The carnage that would result if the market does not go your way can further reduce lifestyle significantly. The other option is to redefine your lifestyle or a combination of all three, maybe. This is how retirement planning is done. We must do the work to have the peace of mind and financial security we all desire. If you are not willing to do the work, the golden years may not be too golden.

Do you have the right financial professional? Do not underestimate the value of seriously considering this question. If you do, you are way ahead of the pack. You have a huge head start. Organizing your assets, understanding the color of your money, and creating a plan for the decumulation, or spending can seem like a daunting and sometimes overwhelming task. The right financial professional will understand the different variables affecting retirement; the difference between Red Money and Green Money, the fact that the earning years are over and retirement is about the income. Retirement type professionals, those that specialize in maximizing assets for income, specialize in providing maximum, dependable retirement income, and peace of mind. Go figure. They are not jacks of all financial trades so to speak. They specialize!

Take a moment to think about your income goals. What is your lifestyle today? What would you like it to be in retirement? Are you happy with your current lifestyle? Is your current income needs being met? Will you need more or less income later? Where will the income come from, as you need more? Some people will have the luxury of maintaining or improving their lifestyle, while others may have to make decisions about what they need versus what they want during their retirement. Keep in mind that money spent for needs provides security and therefore much greater happiness than money spent for the 'extras'.

It is important to find a financial professional you are comfortable with but more importantly one that you are confident will help you make financial decisions that are in your best interest and fall within your comfort zone. Taking steps toward creating a retirement plan is nothing to take lightly. By leveraging tax strategies, properly organizing your assets, and saving and investing in the right financial products that help you meet your income and accumulation needs, you are much more likely to meet your goals, be happy and have satisfaction in retirement. It is important to point out what I mean when I say the right financial products. I mean the ones right for you, not the advisor. You may have a million dollars or more and 'feel' secure, but someone else who has $300,000 and utilizing the right retirement strategy, a plan they can count on, a lifestyle within their means, may very well end up enjoying retirement more than someone with much more money and no plan, or a poor plan. Why? They had a planned approach for that ever so important... retirement asset allocation. They learned about real asset diversification, about Red Money and Green Money and applied what they learned to their assets.

Chapter 10
Takeaways

- There are two types of money: Green and Red. Green Money represents assets that are protected and more reliable. Red Money represents assets that are exposed to risk.
- There are two types of Green Money: Money you need now and money for later. It is important to have assets structured to provide you with income now and later.
- Working with the right financial professional will help you to take an accurate stock of your retirement assets, help you to understand how much they are worth in terms of income, what rules apply to them, and how they are and could be better structured for risk, if need be.
- If all your retirement eggs are in the same basket, whether red or green, you are not diversified. You must have assets in more than one basket. If ones gets knocked off the table, your other eggs are somewhere else, somewhere protect... somewhere safe.

"*Knowing is better than not knowing. Every time.*"

Cassandra Clare

Chapter 11

Risking It All... On Red

In the chapter on risk, we discussed market volatility. We discussed risk in terms of the impact that negative outcomes and bad timing can have on retirees, their lifestyle and happiness. It is not the loss of money we risk, it is the loss of security, peace of mind and the life we hope to live. It is the very possibility of losing our independence and dignity that is at the root of our worry. Now I want to define risk 'management' for retirees. You remember retirement financial planning is all about income, right? It is really, as I have previously stated, income planning that retirees must do, not financial planning. To do that whether by yourself or with the help of a financial professional you must think about and consider all risks that affect the availability of income. Income when, and in the amount you will need it, whether now or 20 years from now. To make that happen there needs to be a plan to minimize or possibly even avoid decisions that can put your needed income at risk. This requires asset diversification between money at risk, which we have referred to as red money, and money that is protected (insured); or green money.

This chapter is about the red money. It is about the money you can afford to take risk with, the money you decide to take risk with. It is about a way to take less risk with the money allocated to risk. It is an option worth your consideration. Some of you may ask, why take any risk at all. The answer is twofold. First, because it provides better and real, true diversification. No matter how much you like anything, even safety and protection (insured assets), by diversifying, and taking some risk, your ability to keep up with and even beat inflation is improved.

Sometimes the financial planning (the INCOME PLANNING) needed by pre-retirees seems daunting. It isn't. It does not need to be difficult even. Do not be discouraged! Once broken down into a step by step process that leads to success, it is surprisingly easier than you think. It will lead to the right asset allocation and a plan for a successful retirement; specific to you and the life you want to live. It can be a plan that meets your needs, a plan you can understand and furthermore a plan you can help create. As a matter of fact, it cannot be created without you. By design it must be a team effort. You must participate. Be very careful of any advisor that has an 'I got this' attitude. I repeat the right plan cannot be created without your help and participation.

There are numerous investment/risk strategies employed in the marketplace today, all of them touting their advantages. It would require a large book; in greater detail than most laypersons would want to read to discuss them all in much detail and that is not our intention. For anyone interested in more than a 5,000-foot level view should do further research. What I want to do here is provide some basics for direction when it comes to risk money investing for retirement. We will talk about three options and it will be an overview, which will be enough for most people to understand the differences. Before I begin it is important to acknowledge that cost is always a consideration when investing in the market. Like all of retirement planning and investing there is no one right way.

Given the option of high fees vs. low fees, we would all opt for low fees. Given more information, say an investment that returned 5% at a cost of .5%, leaving you, the investor a return of 4.5% compared to an investment that returned 9% and cost of 2% leaving you 7%, we all would prefer the latter. That said the cost is for the most part directly related to the time spent managing your investment, the expertise and track record of the manager or managers. It should be known that the goal of strategic type managers, the benchmark is to 'beat the market' or beat the performance of the market. If they do not, then you would be better to not pay for the management. OK, here we go.

So, let us begin with the fact that most managers DO NOT beat the market. Even if they do they are typically not consistent at it. But we pay them to 'try' when we pay for management. The first strategy that has merit and an ever-increasing following is investing your risk money utilizing 'Index Funds'. Simply put an index fund is a non-managed investment in the overall index chosen. There are many and an ever-increasing number of indices; an example of an index used more than any other is the S & P 500 Index. If the market is up 5%, 10% or 20% that is what you earn. If it goes down 5%, 10%, 35% or more... that is what you lose. You lose. Remember there is no truth to "you haven't lost until you sell." This is a slick appeasement created to make you feel better about your loss. Sorry, I got sidetracked. Index funds can be very inexpensive and this is one reason they are quite popular. There are hundreds of index funds. Most of you have heard of Vanguard. Some of you, I am certain even own one or more of John Bogle's Vanguard Funds. They are one of the largest providers of index funds.

The other two main risk-investing directions we will deal with here are 'Strategic' Management and 'Tactical' Management. It is my intention to keep it simple. Strategic Management by design is very specific to attempting to beat the market by picking investments, stocks, bonds and mutual funds that they think will increase in value. The 'strategy' if you will, is dependent on an ever-increasing market and or at least making the right picks that go up in value. Inherent in strategic management is the theory that the more risk taken, the more money you (can) make. Not a strategy I personally follow or believe. I guess you figured that out, since my title is *Risk Less / Spend More*. Earlier we talked about Modern Portfolio Theory developed by Harry Markowitz. Part of the underlying strategy is to 'hopefully' diversify among investments that are unrelated; investments that should not necessarily move in the same direction at the same time. The idea is that you own a 'diversified' portfolio of companies that are in different sectors and different asset classes. The thinking is, that by being invested in companies that are not correlated your portfolio 'should be' safer. An example of that type of management would be, let's say as a manager you think healthcare stocks are a good investment and purchase those for clients. You would choose other investments, say food producers too. They are for the most part unrelated. Now another part of strategic management would include determining based on your time horizon, based on your advisors' assessment of the degree of risk you want, or they think you should have. They also need to determine what percent of each holding you should have.

Again, let me say this is a very over simplified picture. It is valuable to be reminded that the strategic management style was developed many years ago, in the 50's when most people did not even invest in the market. Most financial professionals were much more knowledgeable. There was much less to keep up with. Investing was different, very different. There was no Internet. It was also during those years that the 'buy and hold' became popular and made more sense than today. There were no baby boomers investing their money for retirement in record amounts, in the market. Times have changed drastically but most people today that are counting on someone else to manage their hard-earned money, are still subject to the same old strategic management of yesterday. It is what most financial professionals learn and it is what they do, in one form or another... with your money. They risk it, under the guise of investment. I intentionally am not parsing my words here. Look up the definition of 'gamble' and of 'invest'.

Strategic management is a strategy for allocating assets. It does not employ 'tactical' decision making which is the third strategy and will be discussed momentarily. With strategic management, it is nice to capture the gains in a raging bull market but the rides down are frightening and too frequently erase those hard-earned gains. The way I see it, strategic management can be a roller coaster, not too unlike like index fund investing. We ride the market up and then back down. The only thing that you can do to improve this ride is take better educated 'guesses' to better determine what to buy, what to sell and when. And it has never been shown that anyone is consistently good at those 'guesses' nor the timing of the market. Strategic management also requires that your assets stay invested, working if you will, even in the sliding and even raging bear markets. That is why when the markets head south, financially speaking, you usually head south with them. Interesting that strategic managers make no money if you are not in the market. I hope that is not part of the reason they ride the market on down (with your money).

Another issue I see is that strategic management uses Modern Portfolio Theory and as we learned earlier, it was developed for institutional investors with infinite time horizons. There is inherently a problem using a theory that has no end game, time frame for retirees, for people that have finite time frames. It is called real life. Ah, that eventually ends. Furthermore, maybe the biggest part for most retirees is that the real persons end game plan involves, and even requires you to spend what you have. Again, it is about how best to have income first, growth second. It requires a new understanding, and a new direction. It is a switching of financial gears so to speak, which must be done. By my interpretation, strategic management typically misses this very important point. Any strategy that assumes an infinite life span for a human being is starting out with a very flawed plan. If ya know what I mean. Ha!

Ok, the third risk (market) investing management style we will discuss is Tactical Management. What is it? When it comes to thinking about explaining tactical style it is easier to think in terms of military tactical management. When we think of the military's job, we can say ultimately it is to fight. Now the military could have a strategy thoroughly discussed, designed and well thought out before being put into place. You can attempt to think of every possible outcome, every enemy counter action, you can have a plan for each outcome, a plan to counter the enemy's actions and counter actions, but once the trigger is pulled (pun intended) to implement the strategy, there is no changing course. Unfortunately, investing, preserving hard-earned assets, converting life savings into income can be a lot like making war. Once the action begins things happen that are not foreseen, and are unexpected. Things happen that require mid-action 'tactical' decisions. We can have the best, most expert trainers training our military personnel, preparing them to carry out their defined strategy with precision per their training but once in battle, it is the tactical, real-time decisions that win the war. The military tactical experts make the decisions. We can be significantly prepared with the best military equipment but what do you do mid-battle if we unexpectedly, run out of fuel?

It is the same for our financial retirement planning. The financial tactical experts know that the market does not always go up. It does not always go down. They know they do not know exactly when it is going to go which direction or when. They know that we cannot plan our financial futures around a strategy that requires us to always find the investments that will move up, even in a down market. They know we cannot even plan a secure retirement around finding the investments that won't lose in a down market. They understand and they have a tactical plan how to deal with the market as it unfolds. It can involve holding investments to capture growth in upward swings. They can simultaneously hold investments that will earn you money if the underlying investment goes down in value. They can also make a very tactical decision to be invested in nothing with some or all your money at times when it is prudent. They do not base your financial future on a strategy that requires only upward growth to succeed.

Now coming back to the military example, let me ask you: Do you think there are more military experts teaching men and women how to be good soldiers or more military experts making real time battle decisions in the heat of action? Of course, there are many more experts teaching soldiers how to be good soldiers. The tactical decisions are made but they are relatively few in comparison. The same is true for tactical money management. Something also inherent to tactical management is that it requires more detailed attention to what is happening now! It requires decisions to made based on specifically what is unfolding versus a more generic strategy which requires one to find the 'winners' even in a 'losing' battle, so to speak. The ability to make money in an up upward moving market, a downward moving market and the ability to sit on the sidelines provides, in my opinion, a better option to outdated, strategic management which employs Modern Portfolio Theory that begins with the assumption that we live forever and never need to spend our money. It is a much better way to deal with volatility. Tactical management assumes we have assets that are otherwise invested in 'truly' non-correlated assets. Assets outside of the Wall Street bucket. Tactical management also assumes we can get greater returns by minimizing the drawdowns or losses, than by always trying to find and ride the winners. In other words, have more to spend by losing less, by risking less!

Again, this is not a technical lesson on tactical management. Without getting technical, think of it like this. Tactical money managers attempt to get 75% of the upward swings and avoid 75% of the losses. That can mean that in raging bull markets you don't earn as much, but the potential avoidance of the big losses means you have more money! Isn't that the point? After 2008 I did not have any money invested in the market for a long time. I was gun shy, risk averse, just like so many other baby boomers. When I did get back into the market, I chose to do so using tactical managers. The strategic management I counted on before 2008 failed me miserably, as it did most everyone.

Tactical management is one investment choice, my choice (for me) when it comes to risk. But, it is still risk and this is important to remember. I am still not an advocate for taking risk with money you will need. It is of course, in large part also determined by when you will need those assets. This means you must consider all the other assets you have to live on, including social security, IRAs, 401(k)s, cash, savings, etc. The time frame should be determined and defined by each investor, with or without the help of a financial professional, specific to your assets and risk tolerance. For myself, my time frame is 10 years. I repeat—(my) timeframe. It is for me, for my specific situation and my specific risk tolerance. I am 'reasonably' confident, though it is not guaranteed, that a ten-year period is sufficient time to recover from a big loss. It is based on the ability of my retirement portfolio to take loses and still be useful in the future when I may need the money. Note the use of 'may need the money'. I personally would not risk money I am certain I will need. My 'risk' allocation is likely going to be left to heirs. To make it easier to understand, one should only risk money they are confident they will not need, at least for the time they are comfortable. Comfortable from the standpoint of how long do you think is a safe time period to have the market recover? Remember, you do not want to find yourself in a position of being forced to make that biggest mistake you can make in retirement. I hope by now you remember what it is. DO NOT SPEND MONEY THAT HAS GONE DOWN IN VALUE. I have capitalized this because it is your last chance to learn it in this book. If you are caught off guard and forced to do so, this will likely compromise your future retirement lifestyle significantly.

Tactical financial management, like military tactical management also incorporates the expertise of numerous experts, expert in many different areas before making a decision. It is a team, used to working together to provide their highly technical knowledge and individual knowledge. Tactical money managers typically have years of financial knowledge, algorithms keenly honed over those years and a proven history to justify their cost. When it comes to investing, the truth is, when most people 'feel' the time is good to buy, it is not. That includes most strategic type managers too. Tactical managers are not burdened my emotion. They trust their battle-tested methodologies in the heat of battle. If it requires buying or selling an investment counter to what the market and talking heads are indicating, they do it.

If considering tactical money management for your risk allocation, do your due diligence as you would with any investment. That said, it would likely be done with the help of an Investment Advisory Representative or IAR. IARs are more likely to represent tactical money managers. IARs work with Registered Investment Advisory firms or RIAs. I know, it is confusing. IARs are independent and can do what is best for you. They are fiduciaries; someone required to put your needs first. They are required to have and to advocate for your best interest. This is in contrast to reps or advisors that are employed by a company. This includes most every large financial company that has a name you would recognize. Any financial professional employed by a large company is responsible to the company that pays them, not the client that 'trusts' them. They are required to do what their employers require before what is necessarily best for you.

Lastly, I will end with a couple of facts. Tactical money management is typically the most expensive. It is not guaranteed and the results are not guaranteed. The same as index fund investing, the same as strategic money management, tactically managed money is a risk basket asset. It is an option. Like any financial decision, particularly one you are counting on to sustain you, to provide security and peace of mind for the rest of your life, be sure you understand what you are investing in. Have knowledge of the managers, their management history or track record and lastly, realize that history is no guarantee of future results.

Chapter 11
Takeaways

- Most retirees take way too much risk because they do not know what they do not know. They have only been presented with a one-sided story and know nothing else.
- It is perfectly OK to take risk, to have money invested in a market that goes up, goes down and at least historically has always come back. Be sure you truly understand what risk means (to you) and have a solid foundation for the income you need.
- There is no way to 'know' how much income you can take from a basket of volatile assets or to 'know' if you will run out.
- Strategic management is based on an ever-increasing market. They keep you invested all the way down and then tell you; 'hold on' it always comes back. Strategic type advisors must keep you invested. They get paid based on what is at risk 'in the market'.
- Tactical managers, can grow money in an up market, a down market and also, very important, can go to cash if they feel there is too much uncertainty.

"A real decision is measured by the fact that you've taken action. If there is no action, you haven't truly decided."

—Tony Robbins—

Chapter 12

Taking Charge

Better Now Than Later. Peter Drucker said, "If you want something new, you have to stop doing something old." The responsibility for your financial future lies with you! As retirement gets closer, it becomes more real to you, there is ever increasing concern about whether you will have enough money to maintain your desired lifestyle throughout retirement, no matter how long you live. There are multiple paths your retirement journey can take. You will definitely need the help of a financial professional who can discuss the paths with you, and help you to choose a direction that is right for you, for your particular situation, needs and hopes. Do not leave this to chance and your untrained 'instinct', feelings and emotions. Find someone truly concerned about your needs, someone that listens (oh and hears), someone interested in your retirement ambitions and desires for the rest of your life. Since you will be placing the security for the rest of your life in the hands of this individual, be sure it is someone you can trust. Trust and relationship comfort are critical pieces. If something does not feel right, be sure to discuss it. Make use of your advisor's knowledge and experience. If you are not comfortable with the advisor's advice, if you do not feel you have been heard, don't feel that your best interest is at heart, you must keep looking until you find a financial professional that meets those criteria.

Working as a team, the two of you have a much greater chance of designing a plan that will work to provide what it is you want and need, versus trying it on your own. Once you have done the work together, done the analysis, discussion and homework necessary to put a plan in place, that 'rest of life' roadmap so to speak, then you need to follow the plan, stick with the program. That does not mean that things will not happen, things that will require adjusting when necessary but sticking with the plan is an important part of what will make it work.

It's not all about the money. At the time of this writing I am 62 years old. I am very fortunate. I consider myself to be in above average in health and fitness, possibly well above average. I have yet to meet the 62-year-old I would trade places with specific to those categories. I rarely get sick, I weigh the same as I did in high school, no paunch, I do not take any prescription medications, and except for having my tonsils out, I have never spent the night in a hospital. I still take steps two at a time sometimes, without even thinking about it; I work out routinely with heavy weights (for me, haha!), still do some running, mostly at the beach on the sand (because it is less beating on my joints), shoot some baskets with my boys, throw the football and Frisbee around when I can, and generally still try to do most things I have always done.

What my friends and students do not see alongside this fortunately fit and healthy picture is another evolving (me) that is subtle, powerful and it is something that I am helpless to stop or even slow down very much. For starters, I suspect I have had 'some' mental deterioration. It is subtle and I have no way to quantify it but it progresses, I am certain, as it does for us all. Just to be careful, I find myself beginning conversations more often with, "I am not sure if I have told you this before" just in case I have done so. On the physical side, to my dismay, my elbow hurts for weeks if I try to play racquet sports for more than 30 minutes or so. The last time I went for a 4 mile run (on pavement) with my son, my hip began to hurt and I decided to run through it. No pain, no gain, right? Wrong. It swelled up and I limped for a week. Now I only run on the soft sand. But hey, it's at the beach and usually when the sun is setting. Nice. I have arthritis in my big toe and it hurts like hell sometimes. My lower back can be stiff for days and longer sometimes. It can spasm, out of nowhere or if I sleep too still, I wake up stiff from not moving. MRIs and x-rays have shown measurable spinal stenosis. I get neck pain and stiffness as a result of the same.

Just so you know, I am not complaining, just reporting. I know I am very fortunate. That said, nevertheless, it is a wakeup call; an awareness that I, like everyone have been on this path, my path, headed this direction my whole life. Here I am. Here you are. I knew it would come, just not so fast. I know it will not reverse. As a matter of fact, it is likely to speed up. The good news is, that as a result of the fact I have arrived at 62 in this condition should bode pretty well for the future, comparatively speaking. But, no one knows, right! There is a reason they say, getting old is not for sissies or growing old is not for the faint of heart.

The reality is that every decade of life has its benefits and tradeoffs. I am grateful for the life I have lived thus far. I have many good memories, which I work at focusing on rather than the alternative. I anticipate more good, hopefully much more life to be enjoyed and new memories to make, even still. But it is also a very sobering fact that my 80s will not be as active and creative as my 70s and my 70s will not be as energetic and adventurous as my 60s. Just a fact. As I age, I will be able to do less and then less (OK, shut up, right?). On the bright side, I am self-employed and financially do not have worries. I like what I do, helping people to see the retirement perspective in the proper 'light', and I can continue at the pace I choose. I can make and take more free time than at any time in my life as money is not a concern like in earlier years. But… 'Seizing the Day' certainly seems to be an appropriate phrase for my life right now. I do not want to wait too long to do the things on my 'bucket' list. It is time to get started. This also goes for each and every one of you. Do not put off things you want to do until you are unable to do them.

Retirement is a balance. Without the money needed to provide security, there is no peace of mind and little joy. On the other hand, the life you have left is worth so much more than money. Do not forget to 'spend' your life in a way that brings you maximum value, just as you do with your monetary assets.

As you age, it isn't easy to be yourself in an ageist society. We are constantly bombarded by negative images of aging. We've all been brainwashed to a degree by the culture in which we live and the media that reflect it. We've been told for so long, by so many, what's not possible as we age that few of us know what's really possible. It's never too late to improve our lives. It's never too late to make a difference in the lives of others. It's never too late to chase your dreams and pursue your passions. It's never too late to really live.

There now exists an entirely new life stage—a two-, three- or even four-decade opportunity for meaningful, fulfilling life. This is a life stage that has never before existed in the history of mankind. This is a life stage that can be enjoyed and used to accomplish just about anything by just about anyone. Men and women are starting new businesses in their 80s, taking up new hobbies in their 90s and competing in sporting events in their 100s.

No one is going to be on their deathbed wishing they had more money. We will be wishing we had more time. One chapter of your life is coming to an end and a new one is opening. I hope that your retirement years are filled with all the things you are looking forward to. If there isn't anything you look forward to, get busy and create something! You are never too old to set a new goal, to dream a new dream... and then get busy making it come true. Eleanor Roosevelt said, "Beautiful young people are accidents of nature. But beautiful old people are works of art." Be beautiful!

Epilogue

In Plato's REPUBLIC, he wrote about the great Myth of the Cave, where people were forced to look at mere shadows reflected on the cave walls as their only vision of life and ignorant of the sunlit world beyond their confines. He says that if someone were to free them and lead them up to the light, some of them may well prefer to remain in the darkness. The point is, I am fully aware that what I have set out to teach here, Risk Less Spend More will certainly meet with resistance to some degree, small or large with most people. Change does not come easily. It is hard for us to accept sometimes that what we thought was true, what we believed to be so, is not. We used to believe the earth was flat. We used to believe that the sun rotated around the earth... until we knew better. Someday, in the not too distant future, It will be accepted knowledge that you do not have to take risk to make money. My hope is that this book pushes us as a society, pushes you as an individual toward that conclusion.

The views, strategies, observations and ideas expressed herein are solely those of the author in his private capacity and do not in any way represent the views of either Greenline Associates, Adult Financial Education Alliance, or their respective managers, representatives or employees.

The purpose of this book is not to promote or endorse any specific products or companies. It was written for general education only and is not intended to be construed as Investment, Tax, Legal or Financial Advice. Readers should seek the assistance of a financial professional prior to implementing any of the ideas and strategies taught or discussed in this book.

Hypothetical and/or actual historical returns contained herein are for informational, discussion and illustrative purposes only. They are not intended to be an offer, solicitation, or recommendation. Any representation, discussion or illustration of rates of return are not guaranteed and are for illustrative purposes only. Projected rates do not reflect the actual or expected performance within any example or financial product. Past performance does not guarantee future results.

Although the author and publisher have made every effort to ensure that the information in this book was correct and accurate, the author and publisher do not assume and hereby disclaim any liability to any party for any loss, damage, or disruption caused by errors or omissions, whether such errors or omissions result from negligence, accident, or any other cause.

TOM PENLAND, RICP®
Greenline Associates, CEO/Founder
www.greenlineca.com

Adult Financial Education Alliance, Torrance CA Chapter President
https://myafea.org/chapters/torranceca

Financial Blog
www.risklessspendmore.com

CPSIA information can be obtained
at www.ICGtesting.com
Printed in the USA
FSOW01n1405230118
43711FS